RABBIT
CONTROL

Other books by Jackie Drakeford published by Quiller
The House Lurcher
Working Ferrets
Rabbit Control
The Working Lurcher

by Jackie Drakeford and Mark Elliott
Essential Care for Dogs
Essential Care in the Field

RABBIT
CONTROL

Jackie Drakeford

Quiller

To Jo Lundgren

With many thanks for all the
rabbits!

Copyright © 2002 Jackie Drakeford

First published in the UK in 2002 by Quiller,
an imprint of Quiller Publishing Ltd.

Reprinted 2003, 2004, 2008

British Library Cataloguing-in-Publication Data
A catalogue record for this book
is available from the British Library

ISBN 978 1 904057 01 7

Printed in England by St Edmundsbury Press

Quiller
an imprint of Quiller Publishing Ltd.
Wykey House, Wykey, Shrewsbury, SY4 1JA, England
Tel: 01939 261616 Fax: 01939 261606
E-mail: info@quillerbooks.com
Website: www.countrybooksdirect.com

CONTENTS

Acknowledgements		7
1	History of the Rabbit in Britain	9
2	Know Thine Enemy	20
3	Plague and Pestilence	35
4	Ferreting	42
5	Dusk to Dawn – the ·22 Rifle	64
6	Let the Dog see the Rabbit	73
7	The Art of the Long-netter	88
8	Traps and Snares	100
9	Gas, Fencing and Repellents	114
10	From Field to Table	122
Salute		142
Appendices		143
Index		144

ACKNOWLEDGEMENTS

Special mention is due to the friends who gave advice in their specialist areas, helped with the photographs, and saved the day when I suffered an accident just before the manuscript was complete. Phil Blackman, Rob Moore and the Tredgett family, my warmest thanks to you. All photographs unless specified otherwise are the copyright of Phil Blackman and Jackie Drakeford.

1   HISTORY OF THE RABBIT IN BRITAIN

With the rabbit, familiarity breeds respect. Few other species of non-indigenous mammal could come back from the very brink of extinction the way the rabbit did after the introduction of myxomatosis, and without a finger being lifted to assist it. Indeed the recovery was made in the teeth of its persecution by every meat-eating predator in the country as well as every man's hand being turned against it. Probably only the rat could equal that achievement, and the rat is far less use to us, and has much less appeal than the rabbit.

Gourmet fare for royal banquets, staple of the poor, hero of children's books, bankrupter of farmers, creator of landscape, and a most sporting quarry, the rabbit has been and continues to be many things to many people. But he has not always been here in Britain. His remains indicate that he was part of the pre-Ice Age fauna, but then he fled before the snows and made his home in Spain and Portugal, the old Latin name 'Hispania' meaning 'coast of the rabbit'. The Roman naturalist Strabo mentions that rabbits on the Balearic Islands were such a pest that the Emperor Augustus received a deputation from the islanders demanding military assistance in their control. Soldiers being the same the world over, it is likely that the task was undertaken with great energy and commitment, but unfortunately for our interest, the methods and results were unrecorded.

It is certain that rabbits were introduced here by the Normans after the Conquest, but opinions differ about whether the Romans brought them in previously, and if so, whether they thrived or were destroyed by hungry Britons when the Roman Empire collapsed. The Normans kept rabbits captive in warrens, fenced in like any other stock, usually by wide banks or walls, and from which escapes were inevitable. Yet there is little evidence of rabbits establishing in the wild. It could be that they simply never had the chance, with a host of eager predators ready to enjoy them, rather in the way that a wild pheasant population cannot survive nowadays without remorseless culling of its numerous enemies. The Romans brought the pheasant in, too, and the brown hare *Lepus europeaus*, (sometimes referred to by the older name of *Lepus capensis*) which just shows that, as invaders go, they had the right ideas. Long before the Roman occupation, Britons revered the native blue hare, *Lepus timidus*, which enjoyed the somewhat dubious state of being a cosseted pet or else a sacrificial object in times of duress. Hares and rabbits do not easily occupy the same habitat, of which more later, so it could be that there was too much opposition in those days, and the escapee rabbits never survived long enough to breed. Within the warrens, however, life was such that the rabbits bred and flourished. Known in those days as 'coneys' ('rabette' was the term for a young beast) they have contributed to a host of place-names, and in England you are never far from a coneyhurst, coneygarth, conigree or warren. As well as providing meat that was considered a delicacy, rabbit fur and skin was extensively used by furriers and milliners up until recent times, and I can remember when a rabbit's pelt was worth more than its meat. It always seems such a waste nowadays when I skin rabbits and throw the pelts away, but there is no market for them at present.

The walled-in warrens also provided sport that was considered suitable for ladies, for the rabbits were completely wild, and the warrens could cover a wide area of several thousand acres. Rabbits do not need good pasture in order to thrive, in fact it can be injurious to them, and poor grade land could be put to profitable use by farming rabbits on it. There is an attractive tapestry in the Burrell Collection, Glasgow, of men and women using ferrets, purse nets and small dogs to catch rabbits, and many a lady's lapdog must have shown good sport rabbiting, for such as Italian Greyhounds are feisty little things despite their small size, and even nowadays will eagerly tackle a rabbit.

Rabbit continued to be a prized meat through several hundred years, and warrens were maintained by the ruling classes and the clergy. Rabbit meat had a special importance to the latter, as unborn rabbit foeti, known as 'laurices', were not considered flesh and could therefore be eaten on Fridays and during Lent. With labour cheap and plentiful, and no part of the rabbit that was not marketable – the milliners' and furriers' trimmings were recycled as manure on the land – warrens continued to be an unremarkable feature of the countryside until the nineteenth century, when several events together enabled the rabbit to establish successfully in the wild. Ironically, these changes were all man-made.

Improvements in agriculture meant that marginal land hitherto used for warrens could now grow profitable crops. This was a lot easier than rearing rabbits on it, as a warren had to be managed very skilfully, with regard to feeding, stocking densities and shelter. One of the reasons that rabbits, even when they could escape, would stay in the warren, was that food was provided for them during the hard months; even so, it had to be the right sort of fodder, for too much rich or juicy food would make them scour often to the point of death. Wet-bottomed rabbits will fall victim to fly-strike, which is sadly even today a major cause of death by neglect in the poor 'pet' rabbits kept in foul, stinking hutches at the bottom of the garden. The iridescent-green fly with the whining buzz lays its eggs in the soiled fur, and its maggots burrow into the rabbits' flesh, causing a slow and miserable death. Rabbits occupying the same ground for a few generations will cause a build-up of parasites, both internal and external, and the animals will become sickly and underweight. In short, the raising of rabbits requires as much stockmanship as the raising of any other livestock, and crops are easier to deal with. Next, we had the growing of winter crops, which provided food during the time when previously there had been little in the way of natural forage. And then, with the Enclosures Act, there was a significant increase in hedges and therefore an increase in habitat. No matter how much food is provided, few animals will breed without habitat. In many years of rabbit hunting, I have never seen a hedge without a resident population of rabbits, and in the days when there was a Government subsidy for grubbing out hedges after the Second World War – what sacrilege this seems now in more environmentally aware times! – farmers knew that the rabbits would disappear along with the hedge.

The final benefit was an upsurge in sporting shooting, which in turn meant that a plethora of natural predators such as the stoat, marten and various birds of prey, came under great pressure from gamekeepers. With large numbers of these rabbit-eaters reduced, more young rabbits reached breeding age, and raised more litters in turn. Until the Ground Game Act of 1880 which at last allowed tenant farmers to kill the rabbits (and hares) which were ravaging their crops, only the landowners and their agents had the legal right to harvest the rabbits. Huge numbers were taken, even allowing for exaggeration: in 1874, records from the Ashburnham estate show 10,516 rabbits taken and Thetford Warren, said to have eight miles of walling, averaged 28,886 rabbits in 1855-56 and 1861-62. After the Ground Game Act, farmers found a lucrative sideline in harvesting rabbits and so also did poachers. Various Game Laws starting with the draconian restrictions brought in by the Normans have ever irked the common man struggling to feed his family, and where poaching within a warren was theft any way you looked at it, with rabbits available in such large numbers in the wild, and clearly causing so much damage as they were in the 1800s, it made the yokel's illicit perk of a rabbit here and there quite at odds with the penalties for such a crime. Surely the rabbit sent more people to prison than any other animal: hard labour and deportation followed persistent offences. Yet hunting is in the warp and weft of the English, and even nowadays when few people here are truly hungry, there are many for whom the moonless night and rain in the wind does not mean an evening in front of the telly.

So the rabbit ate and burrowed its way remorselessly through the countryside, destroying crops, barking and killing mature trees, nipping the tops off young saplings, and scalding the close-nibbled turf with its acid urine. Areas such as the South Downs in Sussex were shaped by the grazing of sheep and rabbits equally, long hillsides where the wildflowers and the insect life that flourished on them were dictated by the culinary habits of the conies. By the start of the twentieth century, despite its value dead, the rabbit was present in huge numbers. Michael Home in his book *Autumn Fields* (Methuen, 1944) says that at harvest time, he remembered two hundred rabbits killed out of an eight-acre field. Each man, woman and child that had helped with the harvest would be given a brace of rabbits, which was considered a fair deal.

Rabbit damage in cereal crops

Rabbit damage in maize

Rabbit damage on the South Downs

Effects of rabbit scrapings and acid urine

During the First World War, the rabbit escaped the attentions of the gamekeepers who had gone to serve their country, and this absence also allowed many of its animal predators to flourish, not to mention giving free rein to poachers at a time when meat was scarce and families large, yet still by the 1930s the rabbit population was estimated at fifty million. Hugh Barrett, writing of farming between the Wars in *Early to Rise – A Suffolk Morning* (Faber and Faber, 1967) recollects the uncut last half-acre of a twelve-acre field holding around two hundred rabbits, which were despatched using two hundred and thirty cartridges – fine shooting indeed. During the Second World War, the rabbit was again a staple source of meat, the Government of the day fixing the price at 9d (4p) per pound. More rabbits were poached than ever sold legally; certainly village boys would sometimes be seen walking very strangely with a rabbit down each trouser leg and often one in each sleeve as well. This can get mighty itchy as the fleas depart the cooling bodies of the rabbits and search for more lively accommodation.

By 1951, the rabbit population here was estimated as one hundred million. Families had been raised on it, every young lady aspired to a coat of it, hats and frocks were trimmed with it, crops and forestry were devastated by it. Richard Williamson in his lovely book *The Great Yew Forest* (Macmillan, 1978) refers to a recollection from a Sussex man seeing what he referred to as a herd of rabbits, running tightly packed to their feeding grounds, the mass being estimated as ten to fifteen feet wide and twenty to thirty yards long. Three years later, a healthy wild rabbit would be something to stop and look at.

Rabbit run through standing crop

Sarcoptic mange – although extremely common in foxes, this is seldom seen in rabbits

Myxomatosis was one more weapon in a long tally of anti-rabbit measures, some more ambitious than others. During the time that the map of the world was pink with the British Empire, rabbits had been exported to all manner of places without a thought for their likely effect on the ecology. In Australia, early attempts at introduction failed, but subsequent ones were all too successful, the plague proportions of rabbits in the 1880s being the result of two dozen rabbits introduced thirty years earlier by Thomas Austin. So much for the dangers of inbreeding. Australian rabbits were fenced out, poisoned, and were the subject of early biological control experiments, such as catching them up, killing the does and releasing the bucks, which enchantingly naïve thinking assumed that the remaining bucks would fight each other and over-stress the remaining does. Rabbit-killing diseases such as mange and coccidiosis were also introduced. The rabbits bred heroically, fences fell down or were undermined, the poison killed a lot of animals apart from rabbits (it is still used, and it still does) the mange did not 'take' (wild rabbits are seldom seen with mange) and Australia was too dry for 'coxy'. In 1887, the government of New South Wales offered £25,000 for a solution to the problem, which ten years or so later started as an unremarkable virus, occurring naturally and without great effect in South American rabbits, being isolated in a laboratory in Uruguay. The idea of using it to control rabbits was not mooted until 1927, but it was only in 1936 that field

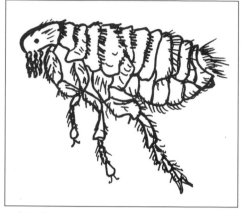

Rabbit flea Spilopsyllus cuniculi

experiments in Australia took place, with but partial success. Several tries later, the disease, myxomatosis, took hold in Australia, and in 1950 an introduction was made that spread to kill millions of rabbits in the next few years.

Back home, an experiment on Skokholm Island in Pembrokeshire was unsuccessful by a strange fluke: in Australia, the main vector of myxomatosis is the mosquito. Over here, it is the rabbit flea. By choosing Skokholm Island, the virologist Sir Charles Martin had chosen an area where neither vector was present in sufficient numbers to spread the disease. However, a French physician, Dr Armand Delille, obtained a strain of myxomatosis from Switzerland, with which he inoculated two rabbits, setting them loose on his estate near Paris late in 1952. By the following March, the disease had spread across France to Germany, Holland, Belgium and Spain. And at about the same time, probably deliberately, the virus was let loose in Kent and East Sussex. There is no doubt that live infected rabbits were transported around the country, which procedure is now illegal. Spread by the mild, wet summer of 1953, the disease claimed a kill rate of ninety-eight per cent, and those who were there speak of burying huge quantities of dead rabbits, of carpets of the dying huddled thick in the fields. While the Ministry of Agriculture dithered about whether and how to confine the disease, or else to let it take its course, the virus proved magnificently unconfineable, pouring like smoke across the countryside. At this stage, the vectoring of the virus was not fully understood; the later studies confirmed the particular nature of the rabbit flea, which needs the blood of the pregnant female rabbit in order to reproduce. Pregnant rabbits are hardly in short supply, but flea stocks have to build up proportionately, which explains the cyclic nature of myxomatosis nowadays.

And so the rabbits were decimated. Warreners ceased to be, ferreters let their stock die out and left their nets to rot, and two generations of lads grew up knowing nothing of the old rabbiting skills. Many people who had enjoyed a regular dish of rabbit refused to eat it any more, though the authorities assured everyone that the myxy virus could not cross species, just as we were assured that DDT was safe, and in later years that organophosphates were also, and that BSE-infected meat was not harmful to eat. Myxy indeed seemed to stay with the rabbit and not spread to other species, which was more luck than science, but like all viruses, it mutated into more and less effective strains. That vital two per cent of surviving rabbits developed immunity, and passed it briefly onto their descendants, just long enough for the young to breed in turn, and gradually rabbit numbers built up. But every autumn, as the fleas reach their peak, so the myxy strikes down the rabbits, and the new generation of rabbiters has to wait in exasperation until two or three months later, to start harvesting the coney. Myxomatosis does not strike everywhere at once; there are usually clean rabbits to be found somewhere for a few weeks after another group succumbs, and the areas and order in which the virus strikes are quite consistent. For instance, where I am on the South Downs, the water meadows and river valleys are the first to get diseased rabbits, then the clay Weald, then the chalk and flint Downland. Some years the kill rate is very high, and in others, the virus just skims off the top of the rabbits and leaves plenty for us. In isolated areas of forestry, the rabbits can escape completely, but wherever the numbers have built up to significant levels, the population will crash again. Rabbits in Australia recovered even faster than in Britain, because the dry climate was much more to their liking, and although you would think that some lessons had been learned from the introduction of myxomatosis, there are still biological control experiments going on there (See Chapter 2).

In about 1997, a new rabbit disease appeared in Europe and Britain in several areas simultaneously. This was initially called Rabbit Viral Haemorrhagic Disease (VHD) later often referred to as Rabbit Calicivirus (RCD). Believed to have originated in China, and been imported accidentally in infected rabbit meat, it spread rapidly among domestic rabbits, particularly show rabbits, and inevitably got into the wild stock a matter of months later. We thought that we faced an even greater plague than myxomatosis, for the kill rate seemed to be one hundred per cent, and once again, large numbers of dead rabbits were found scattered around the countryside. The disease was notifiable, and people were urged to send rabbit carcases to the Ministry of Agriculture, Food and Fisheries (MAFF) for analysis; this was not straightforward, for often there was no visible cause of death, and even with the rabbit opened up, you could not be sure if it had died from VHD – the only way to tell for certain was by laboratory analysis. But the virus was too efficient for its own survival: killing the rabbits in less than twenty-four hours, it had no chance to spread from colony to colony, whereas myxomatosis, taking about three weeks to kill, could travel a long way on a live infected rabbit, particularly as healthy rabbits will drive sick ones out. After a couple of uneasy years, VHD was taken off the notifiable list, and is rarely seen in the countryside now except when it is passed from a tame rabbit to wild ones. Nevertheless, it rattled a warning sabre, and many of us for whom rabbiting is a sublime sport felt that we had come close to a great tragedy.

Rabbits now are largely unappreciated as a food source; relatively few dogs are fed fresh meat, and even fewer housewives are able to skin a rabbit and prepare it for the table. The market for pelts is almost non-existent. The value of the rabbit in maintaining habitat for a small number of increasingly rare insects, and a significant number of wild plants, is generally only known to naturalists. It is a good animal for many species, keeping the pressure off less common food mammals such as voles, and so aiding biodiversity. Nowadays, gamekeepers have neither the time nor the staff to feed their pheasant poults on rabbit ground up with cereals, as was once commonplace. Though farmers without exception detest the rabbit for the enormous damage done to crops, and the undermining effects of the earthworks in banks, ditches and fields, we would be poorer without him. Only as a sporting quarry is the rabbit truly esteemed, but in that arena he stands as a giant. Though it is necessary for huge numbers of rabbits to be killed every year, the skill needed to do this elevates the work to an art form. If you can shoot a running rabbit with a shotgun, if you can stalk them and pick them off in ones and twos with a rifle, if your dog can outrun and out-turn them and scoop them up as they flee, you know about that. If you can set a long-net or purse-net, a trap or a wire, if you can train a hawk or work a ferret or keep upsides of a bobbery pack, then the rabbit already has your respect and admiration, even as you may curse what he has done to your vegetable patch. The rabbit may have come in with foreign invaders, he may be classed as that himself, but his relationship with us is as rich and complex as we allow it to be.

The Law and the Rabbit

The rabbit has a unique position in Law in that it is, at the same time, ground game with the status of game, and vermin, with a legal duty for the occupier of land to take reasonable steps to keep its numbers down. Laws may differ slightly in Scotland, and are always subject to amendment; the lawful rabbiter should bear this in mind and keep abreast of current legislation. The Scottish Countryside Alliance can advise readers and their address is given on page 143.

For further information the reader should read *Fair Game* by Charlie Parkes and John Thornley, and various publications by The Countryside Alliance and the British Association for Shooting and Conservation (see Useful Addresses on page 143).

Poaching Prevention Act 1862 defines the rabbit as 'game' and was amended by **Game Law Amendment Act 1960**. This gives police stop-and-search powers, and powers of confiscation.

Ground Game Act 1880 gives the occupier of land the right to take ground game i.e. rabbits and hares. This law made all the difference to hard-pressed tenant farmers whose crops were being destroyed by ground game that they had not been permitted to take until this time. The occupier may further authorise persons to take ground game provided those persons are resident or employees, otherwise one person only may be authorised specifically to take ground game for reward. The keeping of rabbits caught is deemed reward even if monetary payment does not take place.

1947 Agriculture Act (1948 in Scotland) Agricultural Departments can serve notice on persons requiring them to take action against rabbit infestation.

Pests Act 1954 covers the whole of Britain which, (excepting the City of London, the Scilly Isles, Skokholm Island, Outer Isles and Jura) is designated a Rabbit Clearance Area, and the occupier of any land has a continuous obligation to kill rabbits on that land, or to otherwise prevent damage done by them e.g. by the use of fencing. Under Section 12 of the same Act, it is illegal to spread myxomatosis deliberately.

1967 Forestry Act gives the Forestry Commission the right to authorise suitable persons access for the purpose of destroying rabbits.

1981 Amendment to the Wildlife and Countryside Act gave the occupier of the land or one person authorised by him/her the right to take ground game by night using firearms.

1981 Animal Health Act: Animal By-products Order specifies rules for disposal of animal remains or parts thereof. Technically, it is easy to be in contravention of this Order when disposing of rabbit paunch etc. Amendments have been proposed to address traditional fieldsports and the small amounts of animal matter disposed of in these cases. Be discreet and responsible!

1981 Wildlife and Countryside Act specifies use of traps', snares and other methods. **Amendment 1996** extends the protection from cruelty to domestic animals to include wild mammals. This does not interfere with the killing of wild mammals for pest control purposes provided such killing is 'in a reasonably swift and humane manner'. There is no close season for either the taking or selling of rabbits.

2 KNOW THINE ENEMY

*I*t is the way of the hunter to study the quarry obsessively. Lacking the superior senses of other animals, we are (mostly) in possession of a finer intellect, and therefore success depends on our using this to learn as much about our quarry as we can. We are hunting the animal in its own world, to which it is finely adapted, and in which we are disadvantaged. From this knowledge, this ability to think like the creature we are hunting, comes a deep respect bordering on affection. It is something that a non-hunter will never understand, nor can they ever fathom the addiction of pitting your wits against a wild creature in its own environment. Anyone referring to a rabbit or any other animal as 'helpless' or 'defenceless' displays a most profound ignorance, and though the rabbit is small, big-eyed and fluffy, as a species it has run rings around us and all our engines of war. Rabbits are fascinating beasts: let us find out a little more about them.

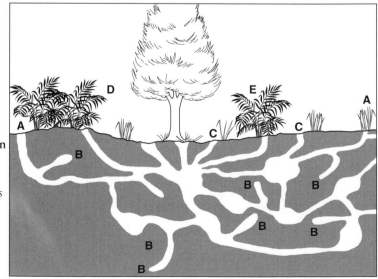

Typical warren layout

A *Concealed exits*
B *Stop-ends*
C *Pop-holes*
D *Exits in thorn and*
E *Nettles*

Rabbits are social animals and live in communities that we call 'warrens'. This gives several sorts of protection: the 'safety in numbers' side of matters being answered by there being so many individuals in a group of rabbits that a predator may be utterly confused by a starburst of rabbits running in all directions, so that it chases first one, then another, and ends up with nothing, or, underground, by a plethora of different and intertwining rabbit scents. Remember that each rabbit smells slightly different from another rabbit. Within the group feeding above ground, individuals will be posted on the outskirts to act as 'guards' and will warn the others of danger by thumping their back legs, or by running into covert. Once running, the rabbit will carry its tail raised to show the white underneath, and the flashing white scuts will warn every rabbit to run for its life.

Being a rabbit is a risky business, and so the social arrangements of the warren are rather fluid, but there will be a dominant buck and doe who will take the best breeding quarters, and the others will occupy the lesser areas. The least favourable places will be occupied by low-status bucks, and the old, sick or weak of either sex, which will be ruthlessly driven out of the main bury. Ferreters often find a small bury with just one rabbit in it, and usually that rabbit is sickly or injured. Rabbits in the early stages of myxomatosis will be found eking out a miserable existence in a draughty open bury when the main colony is snug in the undergrowth. Put a ferret in such a bury and you are likely to have to dig, for sick rabbits seldom bolt. Some rabbits prefer not to live underground at all, and whole communities will colonise favourable habitat such as thick gorse or bramble cover, with very little in the way of rabbit holes except for breeding stops, for rabbit kittens are born underground and a little away from the hurly-burly of the main bury. It is sometimes suggested that the above-ground dwelling rabbit is a recent adaptation, and that these animals are more likely to survive myxomatosis outbreaks, but this is not so.

Mrs Beeton in her *Book Of Household Management* originally published in 1859 refers to four varieties of rabbits: 'warreners' which live underground and whose fur is 'most esteemed', 'parkers' which live a rather effete life on gentlemen's estates and drive away the hares, 'hedgehogs', which live a vagrant life and 'would have a much better coat on his back if he was more settled in his habits', and 'sweethearts' which are tame rabbits. Leaving out the 'sweethearts', the others are interchangeable, for rabbits are far more mobile than most people realise, and whole colonies will up sticks and depart for better quarters when weather conditions or agricultural changes dictate. For instance, during the exceptionally wet conditions of 2000/2001, when heavy rain fell almost constantly from September to March all over the country, rabbits that had escaped myxomatosis and flash floods that drowned others in their buries decamped for high ground and woodland,

Breeding stop

A *Entrance blocked with loose soil and leaves*

B *Nest area lined with wool from chest of female rabbit*

and were hardly seen in their usual haunts. Late in April, they appeared quite suddenly back on farmland as it dried out, and in a matter of weeks, colonies had established again as if they had never been away. If you hunt a particular farm over a period of years, you see how the rabbits leave when the land is ploughed and drilled, to reappear once the crops have struck. There is no sense in living where there is no food, so they move away until normal service has been resumed. It is easy to think that there is a rabbit at the bottom of every rabbit hole, but this is far from the case. Regarding living above ground being safer with regard to myxomatosis, this is an incorrect deduction. Myxy is spread by the rabbit flea, and anyone who keeps dogs or cats knows that they pick up fleas by the score simply by going outside into fields; the fleas live as happily above ground as they do below. Rabbits that live above ground are a greater challenge to the human predator than those which live in buries, though it is great fun trying to get on terms with them.

Inside the warren, tunnels are created and improved upon as the rabbit population expands, and old-established buries can cover a large area both in depth and width. There are the main chambers, the dead-end tunnels called 'blind stops' or 'stop-ends' which might once have been birthing rooms but now are part of the fortifications, and linking tunnels which include steep drops and high shelves, where a rabbit can gain access but something smaller cannot. In land prone to partial flooding, for instance the banks of a brook, some tunnels will run below the water level and then climb upwards again, which enables rabbits to go into the water and out to safety, leaving a smaller predator foiled by the water. This does not work with mink! I have a jill ferret, now retired, which would follow rabbits through these water-locks, but that is exceptional, and I doubt if I will ever own another such. If a rabbit is pursued underground by a stoat, ferret or similar enemy, it will shoulder into the stop and present its rump to the predator.

Concealed pop-hole

The stoat family kills with a bite to the back of the head, which it cannot now reach, and for a rabbit, a scratched and bitten backside is preferable to death. Animals are not known for wasting their time, so before long, the diminutive hunter gives up and goes to find a more obliging dinner. Rabbits also build escape holes known as 'pop-holes' quite some way from the main bury, and often with vertical sides. These emergency exits are frequently in thick cover, or else do not quite reach to the surface, and are a challenge to the ferreter. It can be quite a shock to have a rabbit explode out of a pop-hole in a shower of earth and dead leaves, right at your feet! Most ferreting dogs are very good at finding these, scraping at the light covering of soil or poking a long nose down a concealed exit, and my own have saved me from a great many lost rabbits by these actions.

You may be sure that if there are tree roots then a main part of the bury is lodged under these, where the rabbit has the advantage over a predator by being able to dodge around the roots, and where people, dogs and foxes will have difficulty in digging. Badgers are the exception, for they are astonishingly powerful diggers, and nothing thwarts them. If you come across a nest of baby rabbits that has been dug out, leaving nothing but the soft scattered fluff that the doe plucks out of her breast to line the earth, you can tell what has done the deed by the manner of the digging. A dog or fox will enlarge the existing bury entrance and dig along the hole, but the no-nonsense badger will crown down from the top directly onto the nest.

Crowned down from directly over nest. Typical badger work

Dug along existing tunnel. Fox or dog

Nest Robbers

Rabbits belong to the genus *Lagomorphia*, a small group of animals of which the only other member in this country is the hare. The term relates to their teeth, which sport a double layer of upper incisors. The teeth grow all through the rabbit's life, kept to a functional length by constant chewing. Tame rabbits often have to endure having their teeth clipped, because they do not have access to the rough forage that trims a wild rabbit's teeth. Injury to the incisors results in unequal growth, and sometimes teeth can protrude far out of the mouth, with consequent difficulties in eating. Sometimes rabbits are found which have the teeth growing right round and piercing the face.

As ungulates chew cud, so lagomorphs extract nutrients from their food by a process of faecal reingestion. As with the cud-chewers, this means that a prey animal can fill its belly quickly and then move to a safe area to process its food more thoroughly for the second time. Two types of dropping are produced, the first being soft and moist and never touching the

A Second pair of top incisor teeth behind front pair

ground, for the rabbit curls round and neatly takes the dropping as it is evacuated, to eat and digest it for a second time. The faeces produced at the end of this process, the typical rabbit droppings that we all know, are only ever produced above ground, for rabbits are clean in their buries. Even if they stay underground for several days, they appear not to foul their burrows. Too much wet green food is bad for rabbits, causing severe intestinal upsets, and wild ones will seek out dry coarse grasses to balance this, plus of course their liking for stripping the bark off trees and pruning the tops off saplings which endears them so much to forestry owners. Anyone who has wild rabbits invading the garden knows that they will eat a wide variety of plants, while carefully leaving such as nettles, and the highly toxic ragwort. Wild rabbits get all the moisture that they need from fresh greenery, and only need to drink if this is not available. Remember they come from hotter, drier climes than ours, and suffer much more from damp than heat. Apart from causing chills, pneumonia and parasite infestation, prolonged wetting will strip the soft fur from their feet and faces, and my dogs have caught many such rabbits on the flood plains during extended wet spells.

Rabbits living in sheep country or where there are high concentrations of deer are prone to a parasitical illness called coccidiosis, which shows as creamy spots on the liver. Additionally, they play host to some impressive specimens of tapeworm, which has to infest both a herbivore and a carnivore in order to complete its unpleasant life cycle. There are three species of roundworm which infest the rabbit as well, and for these reasons, rabbit is one of the few meats that I cook before I feed it to my dogs. Cooked rabbit must be taken off the bone before dogs have it, as cooking changes the structure of the bones, and they can either cause impaction in the gut, or else splinter and pierce it – the ultimate posthumous revenge.

Tapeworm cysts under skin of rump, viewed externally

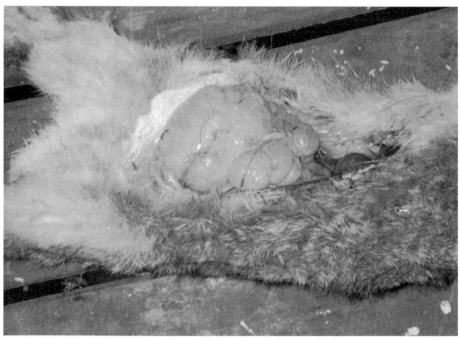

Tapeworm cysts inside abdominal cavity

ABOVE: *Tapeworm cysts rendered harmless by cooking*

RIGHT: *Tapeworm cysts in rabbit liver*

BELOW: *A closer look*

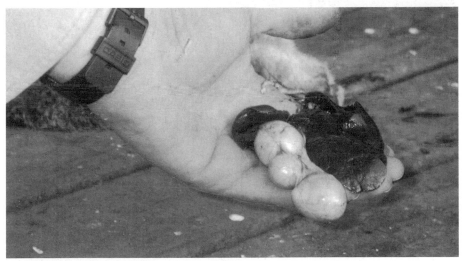

If there is one thing above all that rabbits are famous for, it is breeding. Within the warren, the dominant buck will mate with several does, but the bucks at the bottom of the social order may not get the chance to breed until predation or disease removes the higher ranking males. A doe rabbit will come into season at sixteen weeks old – not much of a childhood, is it? – and will mate again on the same day that she delivers her kittens. In the warmer parts of the country, rabbits breed all year round, and indeed I have caught pregnant does in every month of the year, but the main months for breeding are March to September. Rabbit kittens are born blind and almost hairless after a thirty-day gestation. Litter size is usually four to six, and the doe rabbit suckles them once in a day and then only briefly; I am told by the owner of an animal sanctuary that if you are hand-rearing a rabbit, you must not overfeed it, and once daily is enough; she also recommended using condensed milk as rabbit milk is so rich. Clearly, if you are only fed once a day, the food needs to be very concentrated. At around three weeks old, the rabbit kits start to venture out of the bury into a world full of predators. The rabbit that survives long enough to breed has overcome or avoided many dangers, for a long list of birds and animals eat the young ones: owls, buzzards, hedgehogs, weasels, stoats, mink, otters, badgers, foxes and cats to name just a few. Crows will peck the eyes out of tiny baby rabbits while they are still alive, and I have several times caught such poor infants in my hands and despatched them out of mercy, after the crows have done their repellent work. Doe rabbits often kill a strange litter if they come across it, and bucks will commonly kill their own, though R.M. Lockley in his study of the rabbit (see Bibliography) observed buck rabbits being very tolerant towards youngsters, so, like people, it must depend very much on the individual.

Apart from the obvious way, rabbits can be sexed by the shape of their heads, the does having longer, finer heads and the bucks having a much rounder skull. A mature buck rabbit can be very burly, with a neck as wide as his head, the lagomorph version of a nightclub bouncer. Such bruisers often bear the scars of fights with other rabbits in the shape of ripped ears and scored faces. Rabbits will fight vigorously over territory, which they mark by rubbing the scent glands under their chins onto suitable surfaces. When the

Long head of doe rabbit

Much broader head of buck rabbit

bucks' testes descend at the start of the main breeding season, fights will be frequent, and tufts of rabbit fleck (fur) torn out by savage kicks and bites will tell a tale to an astute observer. Tiny pools of bloody urine show the doe rabbits coming into season, after which it is no more beer and skittles but the hard task of raising family after family. Buck rabbits do not get involved in family life, spending their time defending their territory. As R.M. Lockley says – 'rabbits are so human, or is it humans are so rabbit?'

Even without myxomatosis, the survival rate of the rabbit is very low. It is estimated that seventy-five per cent of kittens die before they are three months old, and of the survivors, less than half will see their first birthday. A two-year-old rabbit has done very well, and very few will make it to the natural span of five years. Apart from environmental disasters such as flooding, wild animals die of disease, starvation or predation, and most rabbits die of predation, though sometimes after they have been weakened by the other options.

Rabbits are generally quiet. Most people have heard the warning thump-thump of the hindfeet that a rabbit will use to warn of danger, and a rabbit

Overgrown lower incisors

in extremis will squeal. Pat Carey in his book *The Ways of the Warrener* relates how he heard a rabbit squeal as it was caught in a snare: the squeal was immediately answered by the croak of a crow. One more reason for visiting a snare-set just before daybreak, and before the crows can wreak evil on the helpless rabbits. A rabbit will squeal when hard-pressed by a pursuing dog, and rabbits hunted by stoats will crouch and bleat in terror, for there is no escape from that savage little predator, who can follow the rabbit anywhere that it will go. Less well known is that rabbits, especially doe rabbits, will growl. I confess that it was not until we had a particularly stroppy doe rabbit as a pet – if Boadicea could ever be described as a pet – that I realised the strange noises I heard while ferreting were the rabbit growling at my ferret rather than the ferret chuntering at the rabbit!

A rabbit is far from helpless in the hostile world that it inhabits. The agouti-coloured fur – a tweed of brown, buff and black – is perfect camouflage, and a rabbit will lie so still that you can walk right over him. Black-tipped ears flat over the russet strip at the back of his neck, he is very difficult to see for those of us with good colour vision, and animal predators will not see him at all, as long as his nerve holds. It is commonly said that a sitting rabbit carries no scent, but anyone watching a fox or a lurcher casting for the whereabouts of a rabbit that has suddenly disappeared, will see that there is certainly scent, perhaps too much scent, for the hunter will sway and rock his head to filter the rabbit smell until some sort of direction is settled upon, and then strike like a rattlesnake to pick the rabbit out of its seat. Humans have so little scenting power that all they can do is make up theories on such matters: my own is that the sitting quarry gives off a cone of scent, and that the predator draws in from the edges of the cone to try and assess where the centre, and therefore the rabbit, can be. Unlike a hare, the sitting rabbit loses its nerve more often than not, the ears swing up and bunny is away.

Those who have only ever seen a rabbit hop will have no idea of just how fast a rabbit can go over a short distance of fifty yards or so, when it has a longdog up its chuff and refuge is in sight. It takes a really good dog to put a bend in a rabbit, never mind catch it, over that kind of distance, though the next fifty yards will see a change in tactics – and rabbits are seldom so far out from refuge during the day. The rabbit can jink and swerve, all at top speed, jump clean over the dog and land running hard in the other direction while the dog sprawls on its side and loses lengths in the process, and will use every obstacle to its advantage, whether running through heavy soil where it will skim through and the dog will sink, or through a fence or gateway that the dog has to leap, whereupon the rabbit will run back through while the dog has to turn and leap again. Straight into farm machinery or dumped rubbish that will injure the dog is a common escape ploy, most dogs will check fleetingly at a patch of nettles or brambles, and beware of the thorn hedge that has been trimmed to leave a gap about four or five inches off the ground, and so will allow the rabbit to skim under and the dog to run into the thorn.

Where is the fox in all this? He has not the speed to chase a fleeing rabbit, so his methods are different, and his skill is in the stalk and pounce, though if he has to, he can turn nearly as well as the rabbit, and considerably better than most dogs. The rabbit is usually aware of what is going on around it, as the ears can swivel in any direction, and are shaped to funnel sound from wherever it comes. The eyes afford vision to the rear as well as either side and the front, there being a small – very small – blind spot directly in front of the rabbit, and an even smaller one directly behind it. The whiffly nose has excellent scenting powers, in common with all wild animals. It is possible to creep up on a rabbit – some dogs are masters of the technique, as are cats and foxes – but you need the wind in your favour, and have to move very slowly, avoiding eye contact at all costs. Once the rabbit's ears are up, so is the game, but it is good fieldcraft to see just how close you can get up to the bunny. Deer are a lot easier.

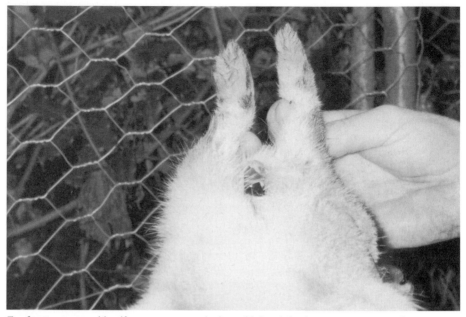

Forefeet (ABOVE) *and hindfeet* (BELOW) *completely padded with fur for quiet movement and protection from harsh surfaces*

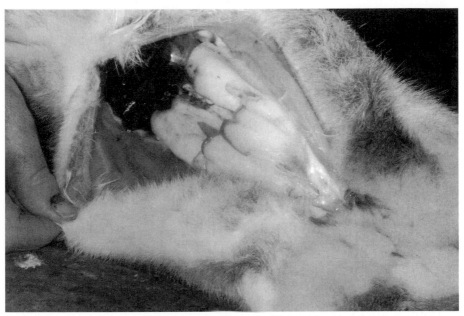

Dense layer of internal fat found in rabbit with plentiful food from growing crops.

Wet ferret shows that rabbit has escaped through water

33

Rabbit feet are thickly furred, enabling them to handle most terrain, and to move absolutely silently when they choose. They can skim over snow, but clay mud finds them out as it balls up in their fur, slows them up, and takes a lot of cleaning. Rabbits can climb quite high in trees that offer sufficient grip, and of course can leap. Some living near me are regularly seen hopping to the top of quite a high garden wall before dropping onto the flowerbeds beneath. Where the wall is at its highest, they hit it as far up as they can, and scramble the rest, rather like police dogs. Less well known is the fact that rabbits can swim – they don't like it much but they are adequate enough as swimmers. A wet rabbit looks really pathetic.

The guard hairs on the rabbit's coat enable it to slide through nettles and thick thorn covert without discomfort, and the downy underfur provides good insulation. They can endure any amount of both heat and cold, as befits a semi-desert beast, but damp conditions are their undoing.

It is not generally realised how well a rabbit can defend itself by kicking and biting. Doe rabbits can do a lot of damage to marauding rats and stoats that come after their young, by kicking them, and indeed there is evidence of does killing small predators in this manner. A baby rabbit might have only four weeks under its mother's protection, but during that time she is a brave defender of her kits. A rabbit's kick is immensely powerful, and a few rakings from the hind claws will make even a human think twice. A rabbit with nothing to lose will bite, and believe me, those chisel teeth can do some damage – I was once bitten in the palm of the hand while ferreting, which resulted in a lot of blood and unladylike language, plus quite a scar. We also have, it pains me to admit, a terrier which has twice been bitten by a rabbit: she knows that the sharp end is dangerous, so tends to get hold of them by the blunt end. Then the sharp end comes round and bites. I have a friend who, while ferreting, had rabbits bolting faster that he could manage, and tucked one between his thighs, still in the net, to deal with as soon as his hands were free. It was a good thing that he had faced it downwards, as it delivered a nasty bite, and he probably still wakes up in a cold sweat at what might have happened.

So, the rabbit can use its camouflage, speed and agility to great effect when evading predators, it has excellent senses, can use the world around it to its advantage by hiding in the sort of undergrowth that many predators would baulk at, or in its underground fortresses, can kick and bite, lives in a social group for mutual safety, and breeds like, well, a rabbit. Hardly what you would call helpless, is it?

3 PLAGUE AND PESTILENCE

*T*he damage that rabbits do is truly awesome. Huge semicircles are eaten out of growing crops, grazing is nibbled as short as a lawn, root vegetables are pulled out and chewed, trees are barked and killed, saplings are nipped off at the top. Then there are the earthworks, which undermine the land and cause the surface to collapse, and leave holes which livestock can put a foot in and break a leg. Rabbits at airfields chew electrical cables and wreak havoc with essential lighting, as well as tunnelling under and weakening tarmac surfaces. Rabbits on racecourses and on training gallops create hazards for the horses; rabbits on golf courses and sports fields create at best problems, at worst, injury. Rabbits change whole landscapes with their acid urine, their destruction of wildflowers, and the way they ruthlessly prevent the regeneration of woodland. Left unchecked, the rabbit creates desert in dry climates, and barren scrub in more temperate areas. Landslip and loss of pasture goes with the work of the rabbit, as well as the more obvious ruin of food grown for human consumption. In areas where they have been allowed to breed unchecked, the rabbit has the status of a furry locust rather than the cute fluffy subject of countless children's books. In truth, our attitude to him is somewhat schizophrenic: a bitter enemy, a

Tree damage caused by rabbits

35

cuddly pal, a sporting quarry. He is all of these, and he is here to stay, for whatever we try, we cannot eradicate him. I suspect that most of us do not wish to do so in any case, but certainly his numbers need to be contained. There is no best way to do this: some methods are more humane than others, some are more environmentally friendly, some more expensive, or more labour-intensive, or require less skill, or certain weather and ground conditions. There are moral and ecological considerations, too.

There is a school of thought which is very common in people who are not in touch with the realities of the countryside, that if you leave everything precisely as it is, it will miraculously balance out and find its own level. Therefore, if you do not kill the foxes, they will kill the rabbits, and the crops will be saved. If you do not kill the rabbits, the foxes will have just enough to eat, and will not take poultry, lambs and piglets. It is a charming theory, and breathtaking in its naivety. To begin with, Nature does not balance; it swings like a pendulum between too little and too much. There are many creatures that eat rabbits, but they eat other things as well; wild animals are as much opportunists as people, and will always go for the easy option, in this case, the easy meal. Anyone who has ever hunted a rabbit knows that the little fellow is a worthy quarry, and no pushover to catch. Therefore, if you allow predators to increase in numbers to put pressure on one prey species, you are putting pressure on all the prey species, some of which may be scarce and vulnerable. If, for instance, there are more foxes, they will eat more voles, which are far easier to catch than rabbits, but scarcer predators, such as owls, depend heavily on the voles, and their own numbers will suffer more as the voles decline within the pressured area. When the foxes have finished the voles, they can move on to other creatures, but by then, the owls may well be unable to raise young because of the scarcity of their own, more limited, food supplies. Within a short time, there will be plenty of foxes and plenty of rabbits, as there always has been, but a serious depletion in owl numbers. That is just one illustration of how you cannot rely on the prey/predator relationship if you wish to reduce the numbers of rabbits. As any Australian farmer will tell you, it just does not work, and a good environmentalist sees that it is far too complex an issue for the glib black-and-white view of 'leave the foxes alone and they will control the rabbits'.

Then we have biological control. A brief history of myxomatosis and Rabbit Viral Haemorrhagic Disease (VHD) has been given in Chapter 1, so let us look more closely at these two alarming examples of germ warfare, and see what they do and why they have failed.

Most of us see the 'myxy' rabbit and hasten to put the poor beast out of its misery. With its bubons and pus, it is a sickening sight; the rabbit takes around three weeks to die, during which time its fleas will infect every other

Wild rabbit with myxomatosis, killed by predator

rabbit that they bite, and the disease spreads remorselessly through the rabbit communities. And yet the rabbit survives as a species – how?

Some years ago we took on four baby rabbits, the product of a liaison between a wild buck and a tame doe that escaped from her hutch to play fast and loose with the boy from the bad side of town. Within a couple of weeks, these weanlings developed pronounced pink rings around their eyes, and we suspected myxomatosis. The veterinary practice to which we went in those days confirmed this, and offered to euthanase the rabbits; having euthanased countless rabbits, we declined the offer, but agreed with the vet to try a course of treatment. We were all pretty sure that this would be a waste of time; in fact it was a most interesting experience, although it pushed the boundaries of what was, in my opinion, humane, right to the limit.

Twice a day, every day, I syringed a measure of vitamins and antibiotics into each tiny mouth. The disease ran its full course: the eyes swelled and closed, full of pus, bubons formed at the base of the ears and in the genital area, mucous membranes swelled and discoloured. Two of the rabbits developed pneumonia, yet none of them stopped eating, and none of them lost weight or seemed to be in any pain. At the height of the illness, I was very much in doubt over whether we should continue, but stockmanship is strong in me, and I felt that, despite their hideous appearance, as long as the

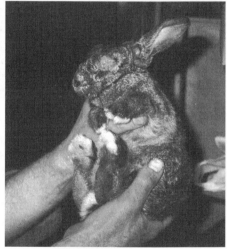

TOP:
Onset of myxomatosis

CENTRE LEFT:
Swellings behind ears

CENTRE RIGHT:
At its worst

RIGHT:
Recovering, but permanently scarred

rabbits ate and seemed comfortable, it was worth trying to save them. Gradually the breathing of the two very poorly ones eased, the boils began to shrink, and the eyes began to open again. They began to struggle when I administered their medicine: a good sign. One more week I treated them, then they were recovered. They retained the typical scarring around the head that you see in rabbits that have survived the 'myxy', and remained immune for the rest of their lives. We have one of them still, a very old lady now, and her daughter by one of her brothers, the product of a moment of inattention on our part and a maximising of opportunity on theirs. Is the daughter also immune? There is only one way to find out, and I do not propose to try it.

If a virus kills its host, then the virus dies also. This is why viruses mutate, and animals develop resistance to those viruses. From the experience that I gained in nursing those baby bunnies, I formed the opinion that 'myxy' by itself does not kill except for the very young, the very old, and the already ailing. A normal rabbit is weakened and incapacitated to the point where it either succumbs to another virus e.g. pneumonia, or parasite infestation, or it becomes an easy meal for a predator. You can hardly call my work with four baby rabbits a conclusive scientific experiment, but it taught me much that I could not have learned any other way, and I feel that, given a food supply, shelter from the weather, and a large slice of luck in respect of predators, a rabbit that is healthy when 'myxy' strikes is as likely to survive it as an average human is to survive influenza. That rabbit now has immunity, and, if female, will pass that immunity to its kittens just long enough for them to survive to breeding age. This is partly why the initial kill rate of myxomatosis was never replicated in subsequent years, the other main reason being that at first the rabbit population was so high that individuals must have been physically weakened by parasites and lack of food, and mentally weakened from stress due to overcrowding. Rabbits are extremely susceptible to stress, which seems surprising in what is otherwise such a tough and streetwise little mammal.

So, half a century after the introduction of myxomatosis, the rabbits are able to survive what in this country is an annual visitation of the virus. The numbers are still reduced, sometimes dramatically so, and they recover within a matter of months. The timing of the 'myxy' epidemics is most unfortunate from both the rabbiters' and the farmers' points of view, for the numbers are cut down in the autumn, just after harvest, when the rabbiters can do most good, and are back up to speed in time to hammer the spring crops, at which time the rabbiters are hard put to make much impression on them. As the rabbit flea increases its numbers, which it cannot do until it has fed on the blood of a pregnant doe, it finally reaches peak concentration at harvest time and another cycle starts.

39

It is a human trait to learn nothing from past mistakes, and a second stab at germ warfare was made in the 1980s, almost exactly a century after Delille released his infected rabbits near Paris. Rabbit Viral Haemorrhagic Disease, as it was initially called, was first reported in China in 1984. It subsequently had a name change to Rabbit Calicivirus (RCD) when it was discovered to be a type of parvovirus; although its origins are obscure, it became known two or three years after canine parvovirus suddenly appeared. It spread with horrifying speed to Europe and Mexico; in its first few months it killed sixty-four million farmed rabbits in Italy alone. Originally spread by imported rabbit meat, and in pet and show rabbits, it was inevitable that it would get into the wild rabbit population, either by accident or design, and it became a notifiable disease in this country when it arrived in the early 1990s. But it was not so easy to trace in wild rabbit communities here, because it killed so rapidly, and largely invisibly in that it is the instinct of a wild animal to die in private. People were urged to send carcases of wild rabbits that seemed to have died for no apparent reason to MAFF for analysis, but not much of this was done, not least for the fact that it is illegal to send corpses through the postal system. It is not possible to tell whether a rabbit has died of RCD without laboratory checks, and wild rabbits that die tend to be eaten within a short time by something or other, so within a couple of years, RCD came off the notifiable list and, while it is still a problem in the pet and show rabbit world, and while it still does appear in wild rabbit communities from time to time, it has not, in this country, become the scourge that we feared when it arrived. One reason for this is largely because it kills so very quickly, and does not easily spread from one rabbit community to another in the way that myxomatosis can. RCD is a highly contagious virus, as you would expect of something that can travel in dead meat. It can carry on the wind, on clothes, through contaminated objects, on birds and animals and their body fluids. The incubation period is one or two days, and it kills within hours of the onset of fever, with few clinical signs. Post-mortem examination shows damage to liver, spleen, intestines and lymphatic tissue, with massive terminal blood clots; there is sometimes a foamy discharge from nose and/or mouth. Reports disagree whether the rabbit is in distress or not. Some young rabbits from five to eight weeks old develop antibodies to the disease and become immune, which immunity passes for a short period to their own young; thus the disease follows a two-year cycle. Like myxomatosis, the virus does not appear to affect other animals.

Unbelievably, the Australian authorities began to experiment with this disease with a view to releasing it into the wild rabbit population. Predictably, the virus escaped from the island laboratory trials in the early 1990s, and proceeded to cut a swathe through the wild rabbits just as myxomatosis had; rumour was rife about human intervention assisting the spread of the disease, but whatever its vectoring, it travelled through the rabbit population with a speed and kill rate that left myxomatosis standing. Surely a combination of these two plagues could not be withstood by the Australian rabbits?

By the end of the twentieth century, there was clear evidence that the virus had begun to mutate, and that the rabbits had begun to acquire sufficient immunity to build up their numbers once more. We humans have been luckier than we deserve by meddling in plague and pestilence in that the viruses still have not crossed species and that they still only infect rabbits. The sweep of the scythe has come unnervingly close – whatever the very real problems of rabbit infestation, this manner of control is not the way forward; twice it has proved conclusively that it does not work, and if we try for it a third time, who knows what devils we may unleash?

4 FERRETING

We do not know for sure when the ferret was domesticated, but certainly the Normans brought them here along with the rabbit. As rabbits will persist in living down holes, it followed that some way was necessary to persuade them to leave their buries, whereupon a number of methods would be used to capture them. No doubt various experiments were made with creatures such as stoats, before the polecat was domesticated for this task. The ferret is closely related to the European polecat, *Mustela putorious*, will crossbreed readily with it, and produce fertile offspring, but these crossbreeds are very nasty indeed, quick, sharp, impossible to hand-tame, and very good at killing rabbits. Ferreters do not want ferrets to kill rabbits: they need ferrets to bolt rabbits. A rabbit killed underground means a dig, which wastes good ferreting time, and a ferret or crossbreed that has lain up with and eaten its fill of rabbit will not work again until it has slept off its meal. I cannot understand why people cross wild polecat into their ferrets unless is it to pick up ribbons in the show ring, for the hybrid is beautifully coloured, with a classic black nose. The first cross is easy to tell from a real ferret, as it is hooded rather than masked; if you want to risk your nose, it also has a distinctive body smell that is quite different from a genuine ferret. Subsequent crosses back to the ferret are much more difficult to distinguish, but regrettably the sharpness of the wild polecat persists for several generations. Rather like crossing a dog with a wolf, or a cat with a Scottish wildcat, the result of crossing a wild polecat with a domestic ferret is an unreliable and unhappy animal. Old-time ferreters further confuse the issue by referring to polecat-coloured ferrets as 'polecats' or 'polecat cross' and white ferrets as 'ferrets', even when, as is often the case, both colours occur in the same litter. The unwary buyer is supposed to accept that the white ones are ferrets and the dark ones are polecats; such is the naivety of mankind that this is often believed implicitly! You may be sure that if both parents were ferrets, all the offspring will be ferrets also. If there is any doubt in the matter, do not buy the animal, as it will be useless for ferreting purposes.

Ferrets come in a variety of colours: as well as the polecat and the albino, there is the sandy, which is light brown and cream, the silver or sterling silver, which has a white body with black guard hairs rather like a reverse silver-fox, the black-eyed white, which is just as it sounds, and variations on grey, brown and white or cream in patches. Any colour will work, but some people prefer light-coloured ferrets as they are easier to see. If, however, you are working ferrets to a hawk, your ferret will have a longer working life if it is a different colour from anything your hawk sees as food. So if you feed your hawk white rats, do not use a white ferret; if she eats mainly rabbits, keep away from the sandies. Once your hawk is used to a particular colour of ferret, always use that colour; there are no guarantees, especially with birds of prey, but it will load the dice in your ferrets' favour.

Female, or jill (bitch) ferrets, are much smaller than male or hob (dog) ferrets, which is called sexual dimorphism. Depending on how you wish to work your ferrets, you may prefer jills to hobs, as most ferreters do, or the reverse. Hobs are easier to handle, though some can get grouchy in the mating season which is March to August. You may not be ferreting during these months, but you still have to handle the ferrets. Jills are sharper and have a stronger hunting instinct – the female really is deadlier than the male – but their prime advantage is in their smaller size, which means that if you are using purse nets, they do not pull them about so much. Hob ferrets have a reputation for killing underground, but if you hunt land that is easy to dig and where buries tend to be shallow, this may not be such a problem as it is where I hunt, which is either clay or chalk, and a real penance to dig. Some hobs are small, some jills are big; small ferrets of either sex are the most popular with ferreters as they are the most versatile.

Ferrets are far better kept nowadays than they were at the height of their use for rabbiting, when their lives were short and miserable. Kept in small, dark, filthy hutches, and fed on bread-and-milk slop, they were lucky to live two seasons. Now, most people recognise the need for whole-carcase feeding to keep a ferret healthy, and they are, for the most part, kept in light, spacious hutches, or even roomy ferret courts. But we must not be too hard on those old ferreters, for they knew no better. They too lived in squalor, and their children were fed on bread-and-milk, as likely as not. It was thought that feeding raw meat made an animal vicious, and indeed those ferrets, hungry and scarcely handled, certainly had a reputation for savagery.

This is all a great contrast to the ferret-keeping of today, where ferrets are fed before work, handled every day of their lives, and worked free of muzzle, cope or line. Then, it was thought that a hungry ferret would work better, but of course the meat-starved ferret would kill the first rabbit that it could, feast on the blood and flesh that it so desperately craved, and then lie-up underground. To prevent this, ferrets were muzzled with either a metal ring or string, or else they were 'coped', an unpleasant practice which involved sewing its lips shut. Even as recently as when I was a child, some ferrets would have their canine teeth snapped off to prevent them killing rabbits. All these methods meant that if the ferret encountered a rat underground, then it could not defend itself, and if it was lost, then it would starve to death. Without the modern locator collar, the only way of tracing a ferret that had been lost underground was to send down a line-ferret, usually a big hob that was kept alone to ensure its bad temper. This ferret would wear a collar to which was attached a line marked or knotted at intervals so that the length used could be assessed. The theory was that the liner would go to the lain-up ferret and drive it off its kill; the ferreter would then ascertain its position by the amount of line that had been paid out, and sink a series of holes until the ferret was found. There was no little skill attached to this, and some people would use a pole in the ground to feel vibration or listen for the ferret. But the line-ferret sometimes caught its line on underground obstacles such as tree roots, or else could not be traced, and probably died a miserable death. There are still people who are well-versed in the art of using a line-ferret, and if you have the chance to go ferreting with one of these, do so, for it is a fascinating experience. But there is no doubt that the best line-ferret is one that wears a locator collar and so has a much better chance of being found. It is a darned sight quicker, too.

A ferret that has had a good supper and a light breakfast of proper flesh food will not stay with a kill but move on to find another rabbit. Ferrets that kill are not popular with most ferreters, so the ones that are bred from tend to be the bolters rather than the killers, though all ferrets will kill underground sometimes. From a survival point of view, a ferret that bolts its rabbits is inefficient compared to one that can kill and therefore eat when it needs to, so a ferret that is lost on a ferreting foray is unlikely to be able to manage to live for long. I have found lost ferrets that were in a desperate state, starving, dehydrated, and covered in ticks so that they looked like small armadillos. Some ferrets do take to a feral existence, but most do not, so if you do have to go home without your ferret, it is vital that you return as soon as possible, and keep on until you find her. It is also an offence to release ferrets into the wild, as they are domestic animals, so you have a legal as well as a moral obligation. If your ferret is lost in an undiggable place, or her collar has stopped working, try holding a newly-paunched rabbit to the hole where you last saw her, which will sometimes bring an errant ferret to the surface. Hitting the bury hard with the flat of your graft will often bring a ferret out, or you can try whistling or calling down the hole, blowing cigarette smoke in, or even setting fire to a ball of paper and pushing it down the hole. If this does not work, you can leave the ferret-carrier right by the rabbit-hole with a small piece of rabbit liver inside; often a lost ferret will be found asleep in its carry-box the next morning. Or you can dig a pit at the entrance to the rabbit-hole and bait it with a piece of liver. Make the pit deeper than a ferret can climb or jump out, and it is likely that you will find it occupied upon your return. Go back at first light, before your wanderer has awoken and gone looking for adventure somewhere else. Prevention being better than cure, be alert to whether your ferrets are getting tired or thirsty, giving them frequent breaks and drinks, and do not put ferrets to ground if it is only an hour or so until dusk. If you stop for lunch when you are ferreting, give the ferrets a good drink of water or milk-and-water (milk alone does not quench thirst) and a small snack of rabbit. Not too much, or she will want to sleep!

Ferreting Equipment

What sort of equipment do you need for ferreting? The basics are locator collars and receiver box, a graft or spade that you are comfortable in using, purse, stop or long-nets according to the way you intend to work, and a carrying box for the ferrets. You will acquire other bits and bobs as you progress, depending on your personal preference. For instance, I like to have secateurs, a swap-hook (sickle), gardening gloves and a lurcher. I recommend that you go out ferreting with as many different people as possible, because everybody does it differently, uses different kit, and will teach you something new. Come to think of it, I learn something new every time I go out in any case.

Locator collars The old-style Mark 1 scollars, which are still preferred by many ferreters, come in eight and fifteen feet depth readings, and which you choose depends on what the buries are like where you work. If the warrens are shallow, eight feet collars are more than enough; if you work hillsides and banks, you will be surprised at how quickly a ferret can go deeper than eight feet. Even though you have no intention of undertaking a fifteen feet dig, it is useful to know where your ferret is, and whether she is moving or still. The locator receiver boxes are a loseable shade of grey, and I recommend using dayglo tape on them so that you do not accidentally bury them on a dig. Always take a spare of each, and spare batteries. If you are working a big bury, a locator box placed at either end can keep you informed of how the action is progressing. A good dog will do this as well.

The new generation of ferret locators began with the Mark 2 system, which had an LED display, and gave out a loud electronic beep instead of the more discreet ticking of the Mark 1 box. There were teething troubles with the Mark 2, which was soon withdrawn from production, and the

(LEFT TO RIGHT): *Mark 1 equipment 15 foot transmitter collar, receiver box, 8 foot transmitter collar*   Mark 3 locator box

locator illustrated (above right) is the Mark 3, again with the modern display and sound. The updated locator is orange on one side, making it 50% less easy to lose, and is apparently very accurate once the ferreter has become accustomed to it. Unfortunately, the Mark 3 ferret collars are synthetic, wider and harder than the Mark 1 collars, and so not nearly as comfortable for ferrets as leather. Nor are they so easy to fit and adjust, though some ferreters have adapted them by incorporating the transmitter into a leather ferret harness, which stays on better and is much easier for the ferret.

The graft This will vary in type with your own preference. Some people like to sharpen the blade for easier digging; if you are ferreting in light soil, the folding versions can be useful, but they are not man enough for anything average to heavy. When you dig, take out as big a plug of turf as you can possibly manage for the first spadeful, and then when you backfill, this can be put back and trodden well in, to leave the bury as tidy as possible. There is never enough soil to backfill, because you have dug into a hole, and you may need to bulk out the infill with stones from the field, or a handy pile of horse droppings. Too much digging spoils a bury for future ferreting, so try to keep it to a minimum unless you are intending to destroy the warren, of which more shortly.

The ferret box This needs to be comfortable for you and for the ferrets. The best are made from fairly lightweight wood, with a broad carrying strap for slinging across the shoulder. If this strap is adjustable, it can be a great asset, as different sized ferreters can carry it in comfort. Some ferret boxes are curved to fit into the waist, and these are really a pleasure to use; remember that you will be carrying that box sometimes for long distances over difficult terrain, as well as your other equipment. If you take more than one ferret, have the box divided into two compartments, and let a wire grille into each so that each ferret can get fresh air. The lids should open upwards and the catches should be easy to operate with one hand: I find bolts are the safest, for remember that any ferret will escape if it gets the opportunity to do so. There are a couple of drawbacks to using the wooden box: one is that

Ferret carriers: single, wire for hot days, double

Ferret carriers: single, double with curved back to fit waist

even the lightest one can get heavy to carry if you are going a long way, another is that the ferrets which are not being worked will scrabble and scratch at the wood and make an irritating noise. People are sometimes tempted to use ferret boxes as seats, which is not what they are built to withstand, and does them no good. But they are warm and dry for the ferrets, and their comfort is important. I have been ferreting with someone who used a metal carrying box which, while durable and lighter than the wooden ones that I use, was cold in the cold weather, hot in the warm weather, and subject to condensation. Damp is very bad for ferrets, as well as

47

being unpleasant. Bedding left in a metal box quickly gets mouldy as well, and of course if the ferrets start to scratch against the sides of a metal box, the noise sets your teeth on edge. Lastly, there is the canvas carrying bag, which is light and does not make so much noise if the ferrets scratch against it, but affords little protection from the weather, feet, or strange dogs. It only takes a moment for a little ferret to be trodden on in its bag, or for

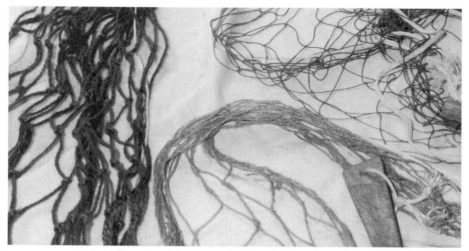

LEFT TO RIGHT: *top quality nylon, thin poor quality hemp, poor quality nylon*

Top quality homemade nets of various weights: nylon, hemp, hemp, nylon, string

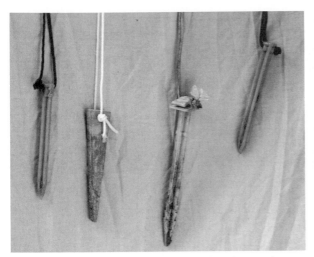

Net pegs (LEFT TO RIGHT): *long plastic, hardwood, serrated-end plastic, short plastic*

(LEFT): *double slider* (RIGHT): *traditional single ring end*

some marauding dog to snatch up the bag and crush it, or indeed for the ties to come undone either through carelessness or fiddling ferret forefeet, and that is the ferret killed or lost. Convenient though the bag is for the human side of the arrangement, it is not safe for the ferret.

Nets There are several sorts of net, and two main materials for them to be made out of. Purse-nets are the choice of most ferreters, and these are placed one over each rabbit hole, with the bottom ring of the net inside the hole, and the peg firmly fixed at the top, either pushed into the soil or tied to a branch or root. If you are netting around a tree full of rabbit holes, a rope around the trunk will give you something easy to fix your nets onto. Pegs can be hardwood, softwood, plastic or metal, factory or home-made. Each will suit a certain type of soil: plastic is lighter than wood, which is lighter than metal, but the metal pegs will penetrate frozen soil easily. Most ferreters use a mixture. Nets can be made of hemp, which is quite heavy, easy to use and disentangle, and must be hung up to dry after use, otherwise the hemp rots. Shop-bought nylon nets are very fine and light, tangle easily and will reduce you to unseemly language if you work thorn country, but need no special care, and last pretty well for ever. Heavier nylon cord is available for those who are clever enough to knit their own nets, does not tangle like the flimsier stuff, and requires no maintenance. If, like me, you are useless at making nets, you will have to find some nice friends who will knit them for you, because you cannot buy these heavy-duty nylon nets over the counter. The number of nets you need varies according to the country that you ferret; warrens are huge here in the

South of England; I never go out with under one hundred nets, frequently use them all, and have to resort to blocking holes with fallen branches, large stones and my coat. I have been ferreting in the Midlands and North when four nets per bury is more than enough.

Sometimes a stop-net can be used instead of or in conjunction with purse-nets, especially where rabbits are likely to run up a ditch, or else you can bisect a hedgerow with them, or use them as long-stops at either end of a bury, where the rabbits will be running for other cover. A stop-net can be twenty-five to fifty yards long, and two of them, or a long-net, can be used to encircle a small bury or else an area of thick undergrowth that is impossible to purse-net. A long-net is generally about one hundred yards long, but the real purpose of the latter is other than ferreting, and will be covered presently. Rabbits will bolt the length of a hedgerow or ditch, and so a well-placed stop-net can be most useful. When encircling buries the process can be quite exasperating, as rabbits tend to flash from hole to hole rather than bolting cleanly, but you will catch a proportion of them. The stop-net is also useful if you are destroying the warren instead of just harvesting the rabbits, this being the only time that you want ferrets to kill underground. Set the net around the bury, then make as much noise as you wish, stamping over the bury and slapping your graft down, shouting and smoking. Using your strong, probably hob, ferrets, send them down and as soon as the collar gives a steady reading, start to dig. I know someone who, closely related to a JCB, always ferrets this way, and brings back some impressive hauls of rabbits. The few that bolt are held in the stop-net, and the amount of disturbance and destruction of the bury means that it will not be used for quite some time afterwards. The last job is to break down or block all the rabbit holes; when they start to be opened up again, you can see at once that the rabbits are coming back. This method can only be used where the digging is reasonably easy, for obvious reasons.

Working Ferrets

For normal ferreting, silence is golden, for you want the rabbits to bolt and not to lurk underground. If the rabbit knows that there is a reception committee waiting above ground, it will choose to stay with the devil it knows, and refuse to leave the bury. So you approach the bury quietly, into the wind if possible, and net up each hole with as little disturbance as you can. Then go and leave the bury to settle for half an hour or so, net up another one or two buries, or go and have a cup of something well away from the warren. If undergrowth needs to be trimmed back before you can set the nets, a pair of secateurs is useful; if clearance on a grand scale is needed, either do it a week or so beforehand, or on the day with a few hours spare before you return to it.

If you clear one day and ferret the next, you may find that the rabbits have been so disturbed by their sudden change in surroundings that they have moved away; a week gives them a chance to settle down and come home again. The disadvantage to this, and it has happened to me many times, is that every village has its old 'character' who does a bit of ferreting here and there, and these old boys are close on psychic when it comes to buries being cleared. If you are unlucky, he will turn up probably for the only time that year and ferret the buries that you have so painfully cleared, to the delight of the landowner, who will probably lose no time in telling you how much better Old Seb has done than you ever have. Old Seb catches rabbits in round figures (thirty, fifty or a hundred) though he never has more than a couple of brace when he leaves, and it is a mystery what happened to the others. I once listened to someone bragging that he had taken a thousand rabbits one weekend off a farm that I, unknown to him, worked on part-time. When I commented on the fact that his car must have ridden low on its axles with that lot on board, he said that he had just left all the rabbits there. A thousand dead rabbits on one hundred and nine acres would have been quite visible, I would have thought, but neither my dog nor I ever found one. You cannot do a thing about the Old Sebs, and it is very disheartening to put in all the groundwork and then find peg holes and footmarks when you come to ferret the land; nowadays I tend to clear

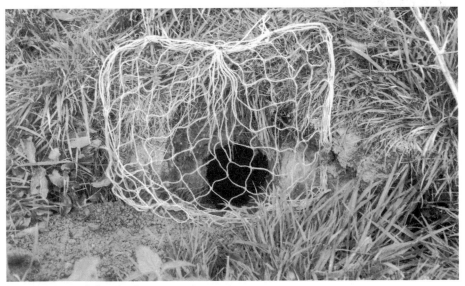

Purse net set over hole in bank

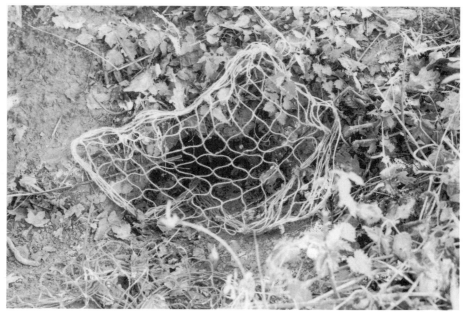

Purse net set over pop-hole

Overlapping sets at adjacent holes

Well-defined rabbit run

undergrowth on the day.

Having netted every rabbit hole that you can find, and left the bury to settle, you then test the ferret's collar one more time, and put the ferret in front of what looks like a well-used rabbit hole, holding the net to one side. The ferret will fluff itself up, gave a shake like a falcon rousing its feathers, and go down the hole. If the ferret refuses to enter the hole, do not force it, but offer it the opportunity to enter another one. Some ferrets do not go down a hole unless they know that a rabbit is close in; others will enter by any hole and do their searching underground. If your ferret backs out hissing, with her tail in flue-brush mode, do not enter her again, for it means that there is something down there of which she is afraid.

Ferret shows at bury entrance

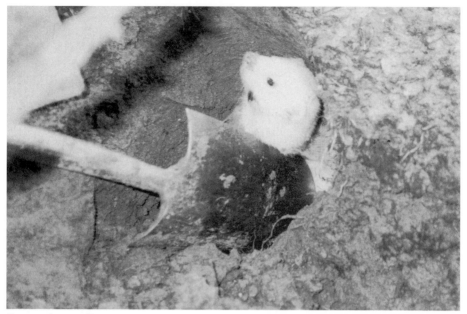

Digging down to ferret

Ferret's reward: a worry of a rabbit carcase

Ferrets don't scare easily, so whatever it is will be something that poses a danger to her. Remember how small she is, and respect her opinion.

If the bury is large, you will need more than one ferret, for the rabbits will really give a single ferret the runaround. Enter each ferret by a different hole, but at the same end of the bury, your aim being to drive the rabbits from one end of the bury to the other. Presently you will hear the rumble of a running rabbit underground, and the whoosh as it somersaults into the net. Lift rabbit and net together, place your foot in the rabbit hole to block it, and get another net over the hole as quickly as possible. Then attend to your netted rabbit and despatch it cleanly, using one of the methods described in detail in Chapter 10.

Ferreting Dog

There are few occasions when I go ferreting without a dog, for the day is much enriched by being shared with a well-trained canine companion. There is, however, no place on a ferreting trip for an untrained dog, which can be a damned nuisance at best, and a danger to your ferrets at worst. 'I'm sure he'll be all right' has heralded the death of many a ferret. A dog must be utterly steady to ferrets before she ever goes ferreting, for the extra excitement will find out any flaws in your training. The dog's job starts with

Dog trained to be steady to ferrets

Lurcher marking inhabited bury

running ahead as you walk to the buries, disturbing any rabbits that are feeding out, and sending them home. One or two may be caught and retrieved to you. If you have seen rabbits run into the buries then you know that there are some in there and it is worth netting-up; often you come to a bury and have no idea whether it is occupied or not, and then the dog's superior senses will tell you. A good marking dog does not paw at the bury or snuffle down the holes, but gently tests for scent and then shows you with a particular look, a wave of the tail perhaps, or, as my old lurcher used to do, by running up and putting her front paws on my shoulders! If the rabbits were particularly plentiful, she would spin around in a little dance, so eager would she be to get going, but never ever did she commit the cardinal sin of digging at the bury and so warning the rabbits that an enemy lurked above.

Any breed of dog will mark, and some people like to ferret with a terrier, spaniel, or even a good mongrel, all of which can chase rabbits back to the buries or show you which ones are inhabited. A trained ferreting dog will find hidden pop-holes for you, and pin rabbits in the net without harming either net or rabbit, until you can get there to deal with them. Dogs love to be taken rabbiting, and the softest family lapdog, the most unlikely spoilt fluffykin, can become a ferreter's extra pair of hands. But only one type of dog is fast enough to catch the rabbit that bolted unseen, or the one that

Lurcher following action underground

Backnetted!

shook off the net, and that is a running dog, usually a lurcher, though I have known whippets, greyhounds and salukis that have all been sterling ferreting dogs. Such is the skill of this type of dog that you can go ferreting without nets and still catch plenty of rabbits, though not as many as if you had every last rabbit hole covered, for Murphy's Law of Rabbiting is that nothing happens and then everything does. The dog treads delicately over the bury, ears flicking, following the underground action through her superior senses of smell and hearing, and by feeling the vibration of the ground through her feet. A rabbit that bolts out of the hole will be snatched up at once by a dog that always seems to have her mouth in the right place; a rabbit that sneaks out ear by ear and foot by foot will never see the dog, frozen into immobility, that watches until her quarry is clear of the bury and then strikes faster that your eye can follow. A rabbit that bolts clear and runs like hell will give a thrilling, twisting course to the next patch of cover, maybe to be neatly picked up in full flight, maybe to get away and live for another day. The times when I have to leave the dog at home, perhaps due to a road or other dangers right by the buries, are never so enjoyable, and are much harder work as well.

Half-time break

Stop-nets

You might have an area of thick cover to work, where the rabbits live above ground, or where the diggings are shallow. One of the ways to handle this situation is to surround the thicket with long-nets and put ferrets in. You will need a lot of ferrets, and it is helpful if they wear bells, not only for you to know where they are, but also because the rabbits will flee from the noise. This type of exercise is best undertaken with as many human helpers as you can muster, so that netted rabbits can be reached and despatched as quickly as possible and stray ferrets caught up before they disappear into the big wide world. Only attempt this if you can have the full area of the undergrowth in sight by your combined forces, or ferrets will escape and be lost. Do not ever mix ferrets and dogs in this type of rabbiting as it may lead to dead ferrets and bitten dogs; a dog bitten by a ferret in the heat of the hunt may well never be steady to ferrets thereafter.

Hawking with Ferrets

The ferret is an important part of a rabbit hawking team as well. A dog will work for you, but ferrets and hawks work for themselves, and the relationship between each is very fragile. Birds of prey tend to dislike dogs, but you are far more likely to have success in rabbit hawking if you have a dog to mark the buries before you enter the ferret. That is the dog's job finished, and it must not enter into any part of the hunt thereafter, which means that, unlike ferreting with purse-nets, any type of dog will not do. This is a specialist task for a specialist animal, and most rabbit hawkers favour a pointer, though some use other gundogs. The dog must be completely steady, must be prepared to hold its point or down/stay for long periods, and never be allowed reward in the form of chasing the rabbit. As the lifespan of the hawk far exceeds the working life of the dog, the handler should choose the same breed when the time for replacement comes, as unless the hawk is exceptional, she will only accept the dog to which she is accustomed. Some very tricky birds will only work alongside their 'own' dog, and refuse to co-operate with others even of the same breed. If you can have a baby hawk and a puppy at the same time, they will get used to each other fairly quickly, but with adults the job requires tact and patience, and they should never be left together unsupervised, no matter how easy they seem with each other. So with the ferret side of the arrangement; stick to the same colour of ferret – the hawk sees the ferret as a meal rather than an enemy, so is not as fussed over individuals as she would be over a dog – and while the ferret should be kept near enough to the hawk that she becomes accustomed to its presence, neither should ever be able to reach the other. Equally so, when the hawk is mantling on her kill, neither ferret nor dog should ever be put in the situation where they could be footed by a jealous raptor.

The goshawk used to be known as the 'kitchen hawk' for her ability to catch meat for the table, but goshawks are not easy birds to train and keep. Most people who hawk rabbits use the Harris hawk nowadays, an American native which, unusually for birds of prey, lives and hunts in a social unit, and thus is much more co-operative with people. They particularly dislike dogs, though, and need careful introduction to a canine hunting companion. Other hawks can be used on rabbits with varying success: the buzzard is quite popular, though better at juvenile rabbits than full-grown ones. You will not be doing that much hawking when the young rabbits are about, for there will be too much in the way of cover and leaf, ferreting will be more difficult because of the nests of baby rabbits, and your bird must go through her moult.

When rabbit hawking, you want the rabbit out in the open, so relatively few buries will serve your purpose. Harris hawks will follow their handler by flying from tree to tree as he walks along, taking a keen interest in the dog below. When the dog marks and the ferret enters the bury, the hawk will be ready, her keen gaze missing nothing. When the rabbit bolts, she is away after it, matching its jinks and turns with incredible skill. She is full of courage, and many a rabbit has been footed by a hawk that has plunged into thick cover after it, or even held at the entrance to the rabbit hole, posing an interesting challenge to the falconer in how to extract the rabbit without damaging the bird, or sustaining damage in turn by a highly excited hawk. Great tact must be used to separate the hawk from her kill, and it is an education to watch the skilled sleight-of-hand used to substitute a morsel of food for the rabbit in such a manner that the hawk does not take offence. A bird of prey is a high-maintenance, exasperating, wonderful hunting companion; you will not catch many rabbits but each one will be the result of a thrilling flight, well-earned, most sporting, and utterly glorious. I have neither the time nor the dedication to own and fly a bird of prey, but I love watching them work, and never turn down an invitation to go hawking. If you want to pursue this sort of hunting, be very sure of the amount of work and worry that you are letting yourself in for, as the ownership of a bird of prey is a huge commitment.

Shooting over Ferrets

Many people shoot over ferrets, and it is indeed fine sport as well as a most effective way of culling rabbits. Safety and fieldcraft are of prime importance, and only areas which are well away from human habitation or footpaths should be hunted in this way. People and stray dogs and cats do not always stick to the paths, and this has to be borne in mind. There is, of course, a lot of time saved as the buries are not netted, and really large buries can be worked in this way. There is no need to clear undergrowth, and no noise or disturbance over the bury, no need to run across it to pick up a rabbit and reset a net. Arrange ground rules before you start so that everybody knows precisely where they are to be in relation to everyone else; too many guns are a disadvantage here, and I personally consider two to be the ideal number, one either side of the hedgerow, ditch or stream along which you are hunting. It is best if one person concentrates solely on working the ferrets, leaving the guns with nothing on their minds but shooting. Rabbits should not be shot until they are clear of the bury, otherwise there is the risk that a ferret might be right behind them. I do not like to see a dog out in this particular situation, unless it is a placid old gundog that can be relied upon to stay at heel no matter what bolts; when the ferrets are taken up at the other end of the bury, the dog can then retrieve the rabbits in safety. According to the wishes of your landowner, other species may be shot as well, for instance rats, grey squirrels, corvids, stoats, mink and foxes If some or all of these are on the quarry list, then you will help the landowner and of course songbirds, gamebirds and the like, whose survival is severely compromised by too much of the wrong sort of animal about. If, however, your permission is solely for rabbits, then stick to the rabbits.

You need a gun with which you are completely comfortable, for the rabbits will bolt unexpectedly and often several at a time. You might consider upgrading to a firearms certificate rather than a shotgun licence if you wish to use a pump-action or automatic weapon, as the latter limits you to a maximum of three cartridges in use at a time – two in the magazine and one in the chamber. This will avoid the frustration of missing rabbits because you cannot reload fast enough. If, however, you are happiest with a standard shotgun, then anything between a .410 and a 12-bore will do your job. Try to place yourself so that you shoot rabbits crossing over in front of you rather than bolting away from you; this presents a bigger target area. You do not want to wound rabbits, so aim for the front end which is more vulnerable. A rabbit shot at the back end may drag itself quite a distance, possibly down a hole, which situation is best avoided. If you need to dig down to a wounded rabbit, or your ferret lies up, be sure that the shooting side of the arrangement stays alert, for often rabbits will bolt when they hear the digging start. Rabbits that do bolt know precisely where they are going – wild animals are not given to random acts – will run much straighter than rabbits that are pursued by dog or hawk, as they are unaware that danger is present other than from the ferret that they have left behind in the bury. They don't run as fast, either, as rabbits that are being chased.

Rabbits that have been shot with a shotgun are usually unsaleable, and can be messy to paunch, but for all that, they offer pounds of good meat which will be more than well received by your dogs, cats and ferrets. Do not worry about the effects of lead shot if it is accidentally eaten; you will be able to remove most of it when you clean the rabbits, ferrets are adept at eating the meat and leaving the shot, and so are cats and most dogs. Whatever is accidentally swallowed is unlikely to do any harm. Once upon a time, it was perfectly legal to sell surplus rabbits privately, as opposed to a butcher or other licensed dealer, and a friend of mine used to supply rabbits ready jointed and neatly packed on a tray. The joints may have come from different rabbits, but there was the right amount of everything, and everyone was happy. The badly shot-up bits went to feed his ferrets, and as we don't eat rabbit heads any more, so did these. Sadly, legislation overtook and did away with this little market; nowadays you would be in contravention of all sorts of hygiene regulations in relation to game dealing,

OPPOSITE AND LEFT:
End of the day ...

and could innocently be setting yourself up for prosecution. Game dealers themselves struggle with ever-increasing red tape, and are unlikely to offer you enough for your rabbits to make the journey over to their premises worthwhile. As good an excuse as any, I feel, for getting another dog to feed!

The Sea Ferret

Before we leave the subject of ferrets, a word about the famous 'sea ferret'. There is an enduring tale of rabbits being bolted from coastal buries by using a large crab, on the back of which is fixed a candle stump. The candle is lighted, and the crab persuaded to scuttle down the rabbit hole, whereupon, you will be assured, terrified rabbits will bolt in all directions. Otherwise normal people will insist that this is fact, and they all used to know someone whose sister's next-door neighbour's uncle's gardener caught hundreds of rabbits just using the old crab and a candle. How you respond to this enthralling tale is entirely up to you; for myself, I can think of far better uses for a large crab.

5 Dusk to Dawn – the ·22 Rifle

One of my friends regards rabbit-stalking as far better sport that deer-stalking. It is, he points out, cheaper, has no close season, does not involve the physical stress or require the physical fitness of hunting a suitable beast on the hill, yet there is a deal of fieldcraft, and probably as much sense of achievement, in stalking a quarry as adept at survival as the rabbit. Active from dusk until dawn, the hour of half-light either side of the night is the best for rabbit-stalking; the dark of the night is for lamping with the rifle, of which more presently. The crepuscular hours turn the most civilised of us feral: we shake off the thin veneer of our artificial world and step into what is for any hunter the time of being truly ourselves. As the light fades, and colour with it, we become acutely aware of scents and sounds. White and yellow wildflowers become almost luminous, and the different shades of green mutate into greys. The rabbit sees well to either side, behind and before, but if you are stalking directly in front of him, and he does not see you move, he is not sure if you are just a strange tree which might or might not be getting taller. You, in the lee of the hedgerow, are stepping softly, one foot in front of the other, perfectly balanced to take your weight on either leg if need be. Though you can shoot with a shotgun for this sort of rabbiting, it is somehow unseemly to shatter the country air with such a very man-made noise; if people are living within close earshot, it is not very neighbourly either. The sound-moderated rifle will do your job with very little disturbance, the greater safety considerations balancing its superior performance.

Remember that background is vital: there must be no people, no buildings, no livestock, no roads or paths behind your intended quarry that a stray bullet could affect, no hard ground or rocky outcrops to give danger of ricochet. Soft earth will absorb your shot safely; though you aim to kill every time, you must choose your background as if for a miss. So you stalk your feeding rabbits with the wind in your face, and your form in the shadows; what will show up is your face, your hands, your head if it is bald or pale-haired, and any blocks of light or dark clothing that are not of the colours of the woods and fields. Be sure that your clothing does not rustle as you move, and, just as you with your inefficient sense of smell can smell things so much better in the chill air, so can the wild creatures smell you, so do not add to those smells that you cannot help with those that you can, of tobacco, sweets, lotions, beer or spicy food. In a group of feeding rabbits, you may be able to pick off two or even three before the others run in, and watch them as they run, for one might pause by the mouth of the bury just long enough for you to take a shot. Once you show yourself to pick the rabbits up, however, the others will see you and all run in. But they will be out again later, and so will you.

Or else you can do the sniper's job, equally effective and less effort, for the rabbits will be coming to you. Seat yourself comfortably, as you may have some time to wait before the rabbits come out to feed. This is a good activity for summer evenings, when it is not too cold to be unmoving. Settled between the warrens and the feeding grounds, with which you will be familiar from your walks around, you will not actually see a rabbit arrive, but suddenly a rabbit will be feeding in front of you. Leave him, for presently he will be joined by another and yet another. The little group of rabbits will be a fascinating study; some will feed, some play, some fight. Choose your target at leisure, and you may get a second shot before they all run in. As well as rabbits, you will see all sorts of wildlife going about their business around you, and you will be the richer for learning as well as for rabbit shooting.

A word about the air rifle is appropriate here. It is my opinion that every youngster who is starting out in shooting should do so with an air rifle. This will teach fieldcraft better than any other way, and yet be more forgiving, for the air rifle demands greater skill and accuracy, yet is less demanding of background than a standard rifle, needing a safe couple of hundred yards or so rather than in excess of a mile. There is a wide choice available nowadays, giving the young shot ample incentive to progress in stages from a standard beginners' weapon to the most powerful, along with all sorts of exciting extras in the form of sights and 'scopes. The top-of-the-range air rifles can be as heavy as, for instance, a ·410 shotgun, and many people who rabbit-shoot as a hobby find that they have neither need nor desire to use anything else. Currently, there is no licensing requirement for an air rifle up to twelve foot pound muzzle energy, providing the user is old enough (over fourteen) but, as ever, legislation is constantly changing, and moves are threatened which will change this arrangement, perhaps raising the age limit to eighteen, and perhaps bringing in some form of restrictive paperwork. I consider this to be a mistaken proposal, for good shooting discipline is easier instilled in a younger person, and should last a lifetime, whereas making responsible young people wait so long before they may shoot achieves nothing except frustration that would be better channelled more positively.

Popular rabbiting air rifles and rifle (LEFT TO RIGHT): *BSA Airsporter air rifle, Theoban high-power air rifle (FAC required), Brno ·22 bolt-action rifle fitted with sound moderater*

Those who flout the law will do so in any case. At the time of writing, however, young people can still look forward to owning and using an air rifle, and making inroads into the rabbit population under proper supervision. Many a child/parent bond is cemented thus.

The use of the air rifle is not just restricted to the young, and many people of all ages find it is exactly what they require for their type of shooting. I know of a hardworking lady farmer whose relaxation it is to drive around the farm in the evening potting unwary rabbits, with her faithful lurcher doing the retrieving, and she did not take up shooting until she was drawing her pension! Half a dozen rabbits a night adds up to a significant amount of pest control over a year, and at far less cost than if using a shotgun, or a rifle which requires a firearms certificate. If, however, you intend to do a lot of rabbit shooting, it

Shotguns
(LEFT TO RIGHT):
·410 bolt-action,
12-bore automatic,
20-bore over-and-
under, 12-bore
side-by-side, ·410
single barrel

would be worth your while to look into getting a firearms certificate, for you could then, if you chose, upgrade to the most powerful air rifles which exceed twelve foot pound limit. These give greater range, and the flexibility of being able to take killing body shots on rabbits (in the heart/lung area) rather than being restricted to head (brain) shots. Though the range safety considerations are greater than for the unrestricted air rifles, they are still far less than for a ·22 rifle, and though the firearms certificate means an increase in bureaucracy and home security, the greater advantages outweigh this – and you are helping to keep civil servants in work, which is always a nice gesture. Legislation is constantly changing, and your friendly local gunshop should be up to date on current requirements, as well as being able to advise on the most suitable gun for an individual – remember how fast young people grow! Yes, the gunshop

Michael Tredgett, competent young Shot

has a vested interest in that it wishes you to buy a gun, but a satisfied customer is a customer for life, and few shooting people possess only one gun.

Leaving a ragged trail in the dew, and carrying a bundle of rabbits, you might have had enough and done enough: at one end of the day and you may have heard the churring of the nightjar or the piercing kee-wick of the little owl, felt the warmth of the day just gone still lingering in a hollow, and watched the stars come out. Or you may have seen a pink and silver sky lift the darkness into dawn, heard the sleepy songbirds twittering into wakefulness before the first blackbird splits the silence with his masterful waterfall of sound, and walked back to civilisation with rabbits at your shoulder and the new sun in your eyes. Regular forays of this nature will make steady inroads into the rabbits, and not leave you in dire danger of falling asleep during meetings as the day progresses. But if you really want to hit the rabbits hard, the job must be done in the dark.

Sometimes the light of the vehicle headlights is enough, or you may wish to use a lamp, which can be powered from the vehicle lighter fitting if need be. You would be wise to use a separate battery pack, as you would for lamping with a dog, if your vehicle battery is suspect! You can take a friend to lamp for you, or do it all on your own. The noise and smell of the vehicle nullifies any noise and smell that you can produce, so you can wear and eat what you like, and I am sure you do not need me to say that drink and

Well-deserved success   *Results of daybreak rabbit-stalking*

shooting do not mix any more than drink and driving; as you are doing both, don't start your evening at the pub. Once on the land, drive slowly, keeping your background in mind at all times, pick out your rabbit or rabbit group, shoot what you can, reload and pick up when you have time. Very large hauls of rabbits can be taken this way, for the others are often not disturbed by their friends and relatives keeling over next to them. Is that a rabbit or a lump of mud? If it raises an ear it is a) not mud and b) aware that you are not nice, and considering running away. If it does not move, it is either mud or a rabbit that will sit tight for you. A single rabbit may lollop uncertainly in, stopping frequently and giving you more than one opportunity to shoot; Lovatt's Law states that two rabbits together will run straight in together in almost every case. If there is light cover, set-aside or stubble, for instance, the rabbits might feel confident enough to sit, which makes life a lot easier for you and rather shorter for them. They will, of course, be correspondingly harder to find once you have shot them, unless they have the decency to turn upside-down and expose their white belly fur.

A lot of misunderstanding exists about shooting from those who have only ever seen death by shooting on television, in that a shot-dead rabbit might kick for quite a few seconds before it lies still, and a brain-shot rabbit can kick itself high into the air, or even down a rabbit-hole. If you have any doubt about whether a rabbit is dead or not, either put a second shot into it or get over to it at once. A rifle-shot rabbit is a clean, saleable carcase, whereas to my mind shotgunned ones are best as animal food. As you are using a lamp, you will be able to see rabbits that you may not want to shoot, for instance you might like to leave the black ones or the juveniles, though my own experience is that the landowners want you to take out every rabbit that you possibly can. You can take a heavy toll of rabbits that have not been lamped before, but by the second or third night out, the survivors will have wised-up, and you will not be able to shoot anything like the numbers of the first trip or two.

Once lamp-shy, rabbits will remember for the rest of that season, and they will teach the young ones to run in as soon as they see a light or hear a vehicle engine. So lamp them hard the first time, leave them a week and really go at them again; if you are lucky you might get a third attempt, but after that you are finished for the next few months as far as night work goes. Do not, therefore, play at the lamping, but really go hard at it when you start, for you will get relatively few strikes at it before the rabbits become too flighty. You will still have the dusk and dawn stalking until a new generation of rabbits grows up that knows nothing of bright lights and vehicles, and indeed it is wise to keep this up, or your landowner, not understanding the finer points and limitations of lamping rabbits, may think that you are no longer doing a good job, and get someone else in. This happens with ferreting as well, and can be exasperating. You, as a hunter, take the trouble to learn about your quarry, but people who suffer the depredations of rabbits are generally too busy or not sufficiently interested to do so. It is therefore always sensible to inform your landowner of what you are doing and why. Take it from me, however, that whatever your good reasons, and however carefully you explain their purpose, what the landowner wants to see is plenty of evidence that you are coming regularly and taking rabbits away by whatever means, and there are always people ready to replace you. Honour among rabbiters means that you do not knowingly 'poach' another's permission, but this can make for awkward moments when you are told that someone used to call but does not come any more, or worse, something on the lines of, 'the ferreters have only been once and said they won't be back until after Christmas'. If one group lamps and another ferrets, this can be quite compatible, but two lots of people

Night shooting. Note the customised rabbit-carrier

doing the same thing at the same time on the same patch of land results in fewer rabbits being caught by everybody as well as a lot of unnecessary upset. Do as you would be done by is the best advice I can offer.

It is easy to become disoriented in the dark, even on land that you have shot for years, so be aware of this and do not make mistakes with the background. Every single time that you shoot, anything, anywhere, with any type of gun, you are an ambassador for the sport. Any episode of carelessness or inconsideration is remembered for ever, while years of perfect behaviour go unremarked. Even with your quiet rifle, the sight of lights on the land can upset neighbours, so it is worth telling them that you will be out shooting beforehand. Be sure to know your boundaries, too, for it is not unknown for a neighbour out shooting his own land to be tempted to look over the fence and see what is out on your stretch of permission. Another potential source of conflict is where there is a landowner and a gamekeeper; if the landowner gives permission for you to be out, always make sure that the 'keeper knows, for he might be out himself, or have given someone else permission. More than once, I have been out with a dog and come across people shooting through this sort of misunderstanding. Once I was out with the gamekeeper at night and the landowner, who was supposed to have been away, had come back early, and apprehended us in no uncertain terms. He was most amused to find that he had caught his own gamekeeper; had I been out there on my own, the explanations might have taken a little longer! To make a success of night shooting, and to leave the land, quarry and neighbourhood in good heart so that you can come back and shoot there again in the future, come and go as discreetly and considerately as you can; this is no time for slamming car doors in the middle of the night, or loud conversations. If your preferred option is going out with a group using shotguns and firing from the back of a pickup, think of the possible annoyance that this may create, and endeavour to finish at a reasonable hour. You can shoot all night with a rifle, and cause little by way of disturbance, in comparison.

The rabbits belong to the landowner, who might be quite happy to let you take them all away with you, or might like a nice brace paunched and hung on the nail by the farmhouse door (watch out for the collie if you do this). One farmer I know likes a couple of young rabbits for the cats, and another likes to take half of the catch. Make sure that your written permission includes mention of removing the catch, because it can be rather tiresome to be stopped on the way home with a car full of circumstantial, and the certain knowledge that if the landowner is disturbed by police enquiries in the wee small hours, he is likely to have a sense of humour failure and that is the end of your permission. Equally, disable your gun before you start your journey out or home, conceal it from view in the vehicle, and have your ammunition well away from it. Your firearms certificate must be to hand at all times. Membership of the British Association for Shooting and Conservation or the Countryside Alliance will help you with any legal problems that might arise while you are out shooting; and personally I believe that all rabbit shooters should belong to both agencies.

Night shooting with a ·22 rifle is one of the best all-round rabbiting methods: you get a lot of rabbits, the carcases in the majority of cases are clean and fit for the most discerning human consumption, the method is one of the most humane, it is challenging sport, and good fun. It will dovetail nicely with ferreting, twilight stalking, roughshooting, and daytime dog work. It is not compatible with lamping using a lurcher, because of rabbits becoming lamp-shy, so what we generally do is have one or two nights with the dog when the rabbits are unaccustomed to associating danger with a bright light, then switch to using a vehicle and a gun. Because the dog work is silent, the rabbits do not initially respond to the vehicle noise when the gun takes over. Other drawbacks are minor, assuming that you already have the right weapons and paperwork; it will cost a little more in fuel, ammunition and licensing, but you can offset this when you sell the rabbits. You will have to clean the car more often, or else be impervious to funny looks from the neighbours and a lingering smell of rabbit (where could that have come from?) and you may find something unpleasant under one of the seats a few days later. You will certainly need at least one extra freezer. Oh, and you will definitely fall asleep in meetings.

6 LET THE DOG SEE THE RABBIT

*P*robably the most versatile rabbit control assistant is the dog, and dogs have been used in pest control and to hunt for the pot ever since they threw their lot in with mankind. Nothing is to be had for nothing, though, and the main drawbacks to the use of the dog are that dogs have to be properly trained, they need a high degree of care and maintenance if they are to function at optimum level, and they have a finite working life with a tendency to break your heart at the end of it. If you are willing to meet these needs and accept these drawbacks, you will find that the use of dogs raises the task of rabbit control to a thrilling addiction. Even if pest control is your living rather than your hobby, you will find a trip out with a dog to be far more enriching than one without, and the whole task elevated beyond mere duty simply from the unalloyed delight of the dog, and your own pleasure and pride in its performance.

Bushing Dogs

Perhaps the area that you are working consists of thick scrub, gorse and bramble or similar, that is ideal shelter for rabbits but difficult to access. Often, the rabbits will be so secure in their thorny fortress that they will live above ground, or in shallow earthworks. With areas like these, it can be productive to encircle the thicket with long-nets, and insert a couple of the sort of short-legged thick-coated tykes that flinch at neither thorn nor nettle. A barely controlled bustle and haroosh will have rabbits flying out in all directions into your nets. It is better if your dogs have been trained to come off the rabbit once it is in the net, otherwise a tangle of dog and rabbit will pull your net down, leaving you watching helplessly as further rabbits ping over the lowered net to safety. Rabbits turning back to cover will be caught by the dogs which, depending on your training and their breeding, will either retrieve or eat them. You might even have the makings of a fight if you are not quick enough about intervention! This is not the way to catch pristine

French rabbit hounds – petits bassets griffons vendeens (PBGV) Darcy and Garbo

PBGV/beagle first crosses from a private pack in Sussex

Some of the rest of the pack

rabbits for the table, but certainly evicts those that you might not otherwise catch, and as a method of making dogs very happy, is hard to beat.

On a larger scale, a pack of small hounds such as beagles, bassets or petit basset griffons vendeens, will skilfully work out a wood that can be surrounded by people with shotguns, and the rabbits can be shot as they cross the clearings. To stand by the woodland and listen to the beautiful cry of the pack as it works its rabbits towards you, sometimes rising to crescendo as a rabbit makes a mistake and turns the wrong way, is a wonderful experience. This is a method that can account for a lot of rabbits, especially if those marked to ground are dug to by one or two people following up the main team. One person works the dogs, the shooting contingent stay where they are placed and are of course very safety-conscious, and the tail-enders do the spadework. Crossbred hounds are often used as they are more biddable than purebreds; one well-known rabbiting professional uses spaniel/beagle crosses, others use terrier/hound crosses, but the pack must work as a pack. This does not apply to the bobbery pack, of which more shortly.

Roughshooting

If you are a roughshooter, a mooch out with the dog generally means a spaniel or labrador. Such a dog will be happy to stay at heel until sent in to covert, will point or mark quarry for you, and stay steady to shot. She will cheerfully push through the thickest undergrowth, revel in water, and her joy is to pursue the runner on a wisp of scent, find and retrieve it back to you. Other dogs will do a roughshooter's job, and some very well indeed, but it is an individual gift. I have seen terriers, collies, poodles and once a corgi, all work to the roughshooter's needs without blemish. If rabbits are above ground, the dog will push them out to run before your gun; if your shot is true, she will tenderly gather the rabbit and return it to you; if, despite your best efforts, the quarry is wounded, a dog is vital in finding and retrieving it for humane despatch. If you miss cleanly, the dog will look at you in such a manner that you will be encouraged to improve your efforts forthwith – like a conscience, only prettier.

But you do not need a gun in order to go rabbiting, and indeed, a lot of landowners restrict shooting on their property, or do not allow it at all. Perhaps the neighbours complain about the bangs, or maybe there are safety considerations. The bullet, once unleashed is unstoppable and indiscriminate; the trained dog is infinitely more controllable. As sentient beings, dogs are never one hundred per cent under control, but a very high standard can be achieved with the lowliest mutt, if only the work is put in. No dog that works should be unreliable around livestock, and should also be steady to poultry, cats, and any wild creatures that are not on your quarry list. Your dog must stop on command, return at once when summoned, and you should be able to call it off anything it considers chasing. If you have

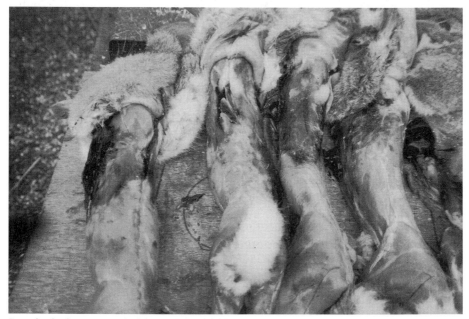

Drawback of using a pack of dogs – bruised rabbit carcases

any doubts, for instance with pet rabbits and guinea pigs, then put the dog on the lead until the risk has passed.

People who do not know dogs generally do not like them, and there is a lot of anti-dog feeling about, for which we working dog owners must take care not to provide further reason. I find it ironic that people expect us to have more control over our dogs, even when they are puppies, than they have over their own children; and even more ironic that we generally manage exactly that. In working dog terms, this means putting in a lot of basic obedience training long before you let the dog meet the rabbit, because once she has found what lies at the end of that marvellous smell, her hunting instincts will surge to the fore, and if you have not laid firm foundations in your relationship with your dog, you may as well save your breath to cool your porridge.

The Lurcher

If you are after chasing a lot of rabbits, the lurcher is the dog for the job. Day or night, the lurcher will find, course and catch rabbits anywhere that a dog is capable of working. The best are velvet-mouthed and retrieve well; at a recent lurcher field trial, the haul over three days and nights was sixty rabbits caught by three dogs. The trials took place over demanding country in the most atrocious weather, and not one rabbit had a mark on it. Yes, you can better that with a ·22 rifle in a few hours at night, but the dog can work where the rifle is unsafe, and I've yet to meet a gun that can retrieve.

The lurcher is a deliberate crossbreed either between a running dog e.g. greyhound, whippet, deerhound, saluki and a working dog e.g. collie, terrier, gundog, or two running dogs (purists call the latter 'longdogs', but I use the term interchangeably, as they are all long dogs). What you have is an intelligent, biddable dog with enough nose to find a rabbit in covert and enough speed to outrun and catch it in the open. There is a strong hunting instinct, and a strong constitution due to the crossbreeding, and different crosses are used because a true working lurcher can find and catch a variety of quarry over all manner of terrain. As we are concentrating on a rabbiting dog, the requirement is at least fifty per cent running dog and preferably more; people who have only seen a rabbit hippity-hop its way to safety can have no idea of the blistering sprinting speed that a rabbit can produce when it has a longdog half a length off its scut. Though some good big rabbiting lurchers exist, and I used to know a giant hound that stood twenty-nine inches at the shoulder and was a excellent rabbit catcher, the best size for an all-round rabbiter is around twenty-three inches. The dog needs to be agile enough to turn with the rabbit, and small enough to catch easily. Think of

Lurcher and terrier working together

the abrupt change in balance needed to run like hell, spin round in a turn and snatch up a fleeing rabbit: it is easier if the dog reaches along rather than stoops down too far. If ferreting is your game, then a very small dog of nineteen inches or so is ideal, for such a hound can pelt through woodland with less chance of injury, and follow the rabbit wherever it chooses to go. If you work steep scarps with rocky outcrops, you will need a different type of dog than if you work heavy clay soil; if you work tight fields with frequent boundaries and no-go areas, you will need something with a terrific take-off kick and instant obedience. For every type of country and every job, there are one or more ingredients that tip the balance towards a specific mixture in your lurcher; rather like a fruit cake, you alter the recipe to suit your taste and avoid what you do not like. The lurcher, as one of my gamekeeper friends once said, is 'any calibre of gun you need'.

We have already looked at the lurcher as a ferreting dog. Most lurchers make good roughshooting dogs, especially if there is a proportion of gundog blood, and many of them, once their more active days are gone, retire happily to work a few more seasons to the gun. I currently have a grand old lady of fourteen who has been a roughshooting dog for the last four years, and is still the best game-finding dog I have ever owned. If the old girl stops and stares at a blade of grass, you may rely on her to be right, and many is the rabbit that the old battleaxe has flushed when younger dogs have passed it by. She might only be able to manage a couple of hours these days, and retrieves are slow and steady, but it makes her feel of value, and has enriched her declining years.

Lamping

A lurcher at night will provide as many rabbits as a ferreting dog by day, if the circumstances are right. The ideal rabbiting night, whether you are long-netting, shooting, or lamping with a longdog, is dark, windy, and maybe with a smattering of rain, for then the rabbits have less chance of seeing or hearing you. When this ideal night comes, my choice is the dog every time. Like many activities, lamping is easy to do badly, which has led some to think that it requires no skill, or is even boring. A well-trained dog and the use of real fieldcraft elevates a lamping night into a sizzling adrenaline trip, oh, and you catch rabbits as well!

In basic terms, you walk around the fields with the dog and get as close to the feeding rabbits as you can. You then shine the lamp, pick out a rabbit, and send the dog after it. The rabbit is not dazzled by the lamp; if it has not been lamped before, it will probably sit tight, in which case the dog will pick it up out of its seat. The dog will find a squatting rabbit difficult to see, and may be guided by a specific whistle, or by rocking the lamp beam. A rabbit that runs will be pursued by the dog, which may follow the beam, swerve out of the light to come at the rabbit from out of the darkness, or work the rabbit away from its refuge by 'goalkeeping' it back out into the open. A catch rate of one in three is a good average if the rabbits are regularly lamped; where they have not been lamped before, higher scores are possible.

In some parts of the country, large hauls of rabbits are made by lamping, especially where there is little human habitation and so less in the way of nocturnal light pollution. A lamping dog needs to be fast and fit in most areas; there are places where rabbits are so plentiful that a relatively slow dog can catch them, or even a dog that stalks along the beam rather than running it. I have even heard of people lamping with a purebred border collie; I have tried this with different collies and I can assure you that they cannot get within half a field of a southern counties rabbit; equally so, a stalking dog would not catch much hereabouts. Different terrain, different dog; if you are thinking about starting lamping, try to go out with a few local people, see the type of dog they use and how it works. Your nearest lurcher club would be a good starting point; people will not take you out with them until they are sure that you are respectable, and when it is your turn to help a newcomer to the game, you will be equally cautious.

The lamping dog runs hard and covers a lot of ground, and it is important not to over-run them, for like mettlesome horses, they have no 'safety stop' and may carry on until they injure themselves. Walking up the sides of fields slipping quietly through gaps and gates, you will feel the night around you like a living thing: your senses will be sharper, and you will be utterly attuned to your early ancestors. Lamping is not a time for noise or company; of necessity it is a silent activity, and at best with just you and your dog, or one like-minded companion. You will wear dark clothes, but not black; it is a curious truth that black shows up in the dark, and you are better with olive drab. Be careful with camouflage gear, for although it fits the bill perfectly, people can get very jumpy about seeing you come and go 'dressed like a terrorist', and you may be reported to the police. The subsequent brouhaha will ruin your night. If you live in an area where there is a lot of trouble with poachers, it is better if you lodge a copy of your written permission to hunt with the local police station, and advise whatever office is open at night where and until approximately what time you will be lamping. It is a minor nuisance compared with the alternative. Personally, I like to wear cammo gear when lamping, but I don't change into it until I am on the land that I intend to hunt. Obviously you always let the landowner know when you are going to be about, but in the case of a landowner who lives elsewhere, or is on holiday, some rather bizarre misunderstandings can occur. I can vouch for the effectiveness of Realtree cammo, and the importance of a lurcher trained to lie absolutely still!

I am sorry to tell you this, but you stink. Rabbits will smell you and hear you a long way away, and you should approach them downwind if possible. Even with this in your favour, the smell of beer, tobacco, peppermints, aftershave, body odour or flatulence will readily be detected by them. Avoid clothes that rustle or chafe, and boots that flubber or squeak as you walk. Tread softly, for the vibrations of your feet on the ground will carry a long way in some soils. Tape over the ends of zips, and the tinkling metal ID tag on your dog's collar, or leave her collar off altogether but remember to put it back on her when you have finished, as it is an offence to have a dog in a public place without a collar and ID. You may have been working her on private land, but your car is deemed a public place; remember the pit-bull terrier that was condemned to death because its owner had it unmuzzled in his own car? There are those who would stoop thus low to have your dog confiscated, too, and you would be unlikely to get her back. If you have pale hair or none, wear a hat; I regularly meet a roughshooter who comes out in expensive camouflage, but you can see his bright silver hair for quite a distance.

Though the windy, moonless night is ideal, you will seldom go out lamping if you wait for these conditions; personally I find a light windy night to be better than a still dark one, and if you have the choice of approaching right for the wind or right for the land, go for the land, hugging its contours and being careful not to shine your lamp over the brow of the hill, and to keep below it yourself. Do not send your dog until you are sure that your quarry is a rabbit; a little owl, partridge, or the old farm cat can all look surprisingly like rabbits if that is what you are expecting to see.

Lamping equipment is simple, especially nowadays when there is quite a choice of lamps to buy. In the old days, people used car batteries wired into old headlamps, the battery carried in a cut-down polythene container on their backs, to avoid spilling acid down their clothes. Some die-hards still do this: it is not expensive if the basics are taken from a scrapyard. It is, however, heavy and cumbersome. The factory-made lamps are much more comfortable to carry, though no battery pack that can put out the candlepower of a hunting lamp could be described as light. Shoulder packs are the most usual; I use a belt pack as I am not strong across the shoulders, and find it much more comfortable. A slender man would find a combination of the two preferable, as, lacking the curve of feminine hips, there is little for the belt batteries to sit upon without the extra support of the shoulder strap. The resulting slow descent of the batteries otherwise has a tendency to take trousers with it, and cause unseemly mirth in one's lamping colleague. I have

A well-used lamp and belt battery pack

tried carrying the battery pack in a rucksack on my back, but this is an extra complication if there are wire fences to climb through.

How do you carry your rabbits? Again, the rucksack is an option in open country, or there is a variety of gamebags and game carriers, or you can pause every now and then to hock and hang the rabbits on fences, which will mean that you have to return the way you came, and also that some rabbits will not be there when you do, just a lingering whiff of fox instead. Quite a few hunters are superstitious about using a gamebag; certainly a new one seems to be the best way I know of ensuring a blank day. If you are the only one with a gamebag, you will end up carrying all the rabbits, which is no fun either. The best rabbit carrier is someone else; in the absence of this, I wear jackets or waistcoats with plenty of deep pockets. In the old days, rabbiters would have coats which were lined on the inside to be all pocket, which must have been very cosy when filled.

Purists say that a lamping lurcher should work at all times off the slip, but many dogs are so keen that a slip has to be used. For night work, the complex coursing slip is no use: instead, a simple length of soft rope, or a dog lead with the clip cut off makes a perfectly adequate slip. Baler twine (binder band) is best avoided as it will cut your fingers if the dog pulls. Never mind about purists; if using a slip makes the difference between a relaxing lamping trip and a stressful one, use the slip. It is a matter between yourself and your dog, and nobody else's business at all.

Always check by day any land that you are working by night, and always advise your landowner, for livestock may have been moved, fencing may have been altered, and farm machinery may have been left in a place where your dog can run into it, or leap a fence and

The best rabbit carrier is somebody else! Jim Lyons from Berkshire, always ready to help

land on top of it. Neighbours may need to know that you are about, and might even ask if you will hunt their property as well.

Hunting in Packs

Dogs by nature like to hunt in packs, and for rabbit catching, this instinct can be harnessed using a formal pack or a bobbery pack. Formal packs tend to use a specific breed of hound or crossbred hound, most usually small bassets or beagles, and operate much in the same way as foxhound or beagle packs, save that the rabbit is the main quarry. Rabbit hunters are not too worried if their pack 'riots' on such as mink, rat, stoat or fox, for all these species need to be kept in check, but the rabbit is their raison d'etre. One of the best known of the formal rabbit packs is the Ryford Chase in Herefordshire, which consists at time of writing of thirty couple of griffon vendeen bassets and four couple of working teckels (working-bred wire-haired dachshunds); in the recent past, it was not unknown for the odd lurcher or bull terrier cross to be allowed to join. The Ryford Chase is a registered private pack with proper Hunt livery and etiquette, the quarry is rabbits and hares, and it has been in existence since 1974. Another smart rabbit pack is Brian Plummer's Raggengill pack, consisting primarily of Lucas terriers. Brian is well known for his dog training skills, and has hunted successfully with his own Plummer terriers, Sealyhams, and even show-bred Cavalier King Charles spaniels, as well as the Lucas. There are many other rabbit packs run by enthusiasts, usually with the basset or beagle base to give a smallish hound with good nose, voice and packing instinct. Any dog will hunt, but some breeds 'pack' better than others, and if you are running terriers that have not had an outcross of hound blood, you can end up with each terrier doing its own thing, and fourteen different hunts going on instead of seven couple on one rabbit. If you use a family group, you are less likely to have this, for the dog or wolf pack is not a series of unrelated canids that met in the woods one day, but an extended family. The bitch will teach the pups to hunt, and you will have a pack, but beware, for you will be on a knife edge of control unless the senior dogs are completely steady. Any hint of insubordination must be instantly and firmly quelled, and no dog must exceed your authority. With terriers especially, believe me, they will try to.

The Bobbery Pack
The origin of the word 'bobbery' is in some dispute, but is generally thought to be Indian in origin, dating from the time of the Raj, and to be a

Bobbery pack – three lurchers waiting; scenthounds working in covert

corruption of an expression of amused dismay. Most bobbery packs consist of whatever is to hand on the day. I have hunted with all sorts and mixtures, and would only say that it is useful to have at least one hound for the scenting and giving tongue, a lurcher for the sprinting work, a terrier or two for squeezing into tight places and entering thick covert, and a retired gundog for retrieving and to lend an air of respectability. I say retired because this sort of thing will thoroughly unsteady a gundog which is expected to sit politely and silently at a peg or in a hide until given the office to 'go'. Dachshunds are hound and terrier in one, wonderful little hunting dogs but not the most biddable, collies are versatile but can spend more time trying to round up the other dogs than actually doing anything useful, terriers have a tendency to scrap, and specialise in the internal retrieve, and a nice old mongrel from the dogs' home might turn out to be the best of them all. This lower end of the scale can be terrific fun and account for quite a few rabbits but will be informal and require a degree of flexibility and sense of humour, more in the style of the fabled 'Bagley Rat Hounds' – immortalised in a series of articles in the 1950s, by that great hunting character and writer, Jack Ivester Lloyd. The pack of rabbiting dogs will also cause sufficient disturbance on a regular basis to keep the rabbits moving, and deter incomers from settling, while having little or no negative effect on the other species and the environment. What you will not have is rabbit for dinner, not unless you are an exceptional athlete and don't have too many terriers, for the kill will be divided up and eaten long before you can get there in the majority of cases. A pack of rabbit hounds is ideal in areas of thick covert that are punctuated by open spaces, reed beds or hedgerow, and it is an education to watch dogs that are hunted regularly together working as a team. You can even take a man with a gun as backstop, but make sure that you choose someone who is not going to shoot a rabbit off the end of a dog's nose. Only rabbits that bolt back while the pack is engaged with another may be shot; otherwise leave the gun at home.

It is interesting to note pack hierarchy, and how matters alter when a new dog is added to the pack. I have hunted many bobbery packs over the years, and when the same dogs hunt together regularly, they use each other's strengths most positively. For instance, if my old dog marks, the others will follow her at once, but if the sassy young terrier starts working, they will only react once she starts to give tongue, for she is apt to dwell on old scent. The 'pack leader' is almost always a mature bitch, but in fact the pack is a fluid and democratic arrangement for the most part, with every member getting its fifteen minutes of fame. If a new dog is added, or I take one or more of mine to join a friend's pack, it does not take long before the newcomer's skills have been assessed, and it fits seamlessly into the team. A bobbery pack works best with one human in charge, but some dogs will only work to their owner, and some dogs will never pack at all. Our Lakeland terrier was an independent cuss, and would never co operate with the others, usually doing her own thing some hundred yards adrift of the main action. However, this did result in some spectacular courses for the lurchers, as the old hag would often bolt a rabbit at some distance from the main pack, a rabbit that might otherwise have sat tight or gone below ground. It is mildly exasperating to have longdogs thrashing out the undergrowth and terriers bouncing about in the open when the reverse is much more efficient, but a bobbery pack is not for the serious-minded. Though there is no doubt that it can make quite a dent in the rabbit population, and is very effective at culling the weak, sick, old and stupid, which is good management by any standard.

The Moocher's Dog

Leaving aside the work of the long-netter's dog, which will be covered in Chapter 7, the other main method of catching rabbits using dogs involves a single lurcher and her handler just going for a mooch around the woods and fields. Quite the opposite of the noise, dash and scurry and triumphant kill of the bobbery pack is the silent running dog, that covers the ground at a

A single lurcher retrieves to hand …

deceptive trot, head now high for air scent, now low for ground scent, scanning the distance with her keen eyes, diving to pick the unseen rabbit out of its squat, freezing like a pointer to show the rabbit hidden in the brambles, creeping low like a cat, or tall, with a jerky clockwork motion that gets her so close to the feeding rabbits before her final sprint. She may come back as fast as she went out, rabbit held high but quite undamaged in her long jaws, or she may miss and canter back to heel until you send her forth again with a sweep of your arm. Walking

… and spies the next rabbit

86

with her is a constant stream of communication, though you may not say a word, and she will not utter a sound. Greyhounds are faster, collies more tractable, terriers might be feistier, or a labrador more patient; nothing but a lurcher can do a lurcher's job. For so long she was reviled as the poachers' or travellers' companion, yet her skills mean that her owner can work with the law instead of aside from it. As a pest controllers' companion, the lurcher is in a class of her own. Though this evening you have only been for a walk around the farm where the farmer has mentioned that the rabbits are on the increase again, you seem to be carrying rabbits, and she has just floated over the stile with another bunny held lightly in her mouth. A gundog for the gun, a terrier for underground, a merry pack of hounds for voice and nosework, these cannot be bettered. But for an all-round rabbit finder and rabbit catcher, the lurcher is the dog for me.

A fine morning's work. 'Charlie' with his first rabbit

7 THE ART OF THE LONG-NETTER

Almost every rabbiter has had a try at long-netting, and a great many long-nets languish, unused, at the backs of garden sheds, following their few attempts at this art. The romance of the long-net is a compelling one, and every book of old poachers' reminiscences is full of tales of derring-do that involve the setting of long-nets on dark, windy nights, and the catching of hundreds of rabbits thereby. There are excellent long-netting demonstrations at country shows, and one or two videos, that make it all look so easy. And yet for most novice long-netters, the reality is a frustrating failure. What can be going wrong?

First of all, a look at the equipment will be beneficial. The old poachers of a hundred years ago knitted their own nets, usually of silk, which is light, tough and long-lasting. Indeed, Brian Brinded, who gives such excellent

Encircling thick woodland scrub with a long-net

Stop-net in summer

demonstrations of long-netting at shows, is still using one of these silk nets. Confiscation of his nets was a more serious matter even than the shooting of his dog for one of the poachers of days gone by, for the materials were expensive, and the nets took a long time to make for someone who was working from dawn until dusk. The net itself is no less than fifty and no more than one hundred yards long, three to four feet wide, with a draw-cord at top and bottom, and pegged every few yards with stakes about two feet six inches high. The bottom of the net must have plenty of 'bag' to it – known as 'kill' – which is where the bought nylon nets that you can get nowadays are somewhat lacking. The 'kill' is what catches the rabbits; with insufficient slack at the bottom of the net, the rabbits bounce off into freedom again. If you do buy your nets, it is worth customising them so that you have a lot more kill in the bottom than has been allowed in the original net, which means buying a longer length and shortening the top drawcord.

Traditionally, the stakes were made of hazel-wood, sharpened to a point at one end for ease of setting into the ground, and with the top couple of inches peeled, so that you can see it better in the dark. Hazel is good to use but will not drive into hard ground with ease; metal will, but is heavy to carry and noisy to use. I find that plastic or fibreglass electric-fence stakes with a metal point at the bottom are light, no noisier than wood, easy to use and maintenance-free; lacking the roughness of wood, they will allow the

Setting up a long-net

One of the ways of securing the top of the net – traditional hazel pegs in use here

net to slip down if the person setting the stakes has been careless, but this is easily remedied with a strip of tape near the top where you want the net to sit. Traditionally, stakes and net are carried separately, but of recent years, it has become the norm to have the stakes permanently attached to the net. If you choose this method, which I find easier and more convenient than the traditional manner, the two end stakes are fed through the mesh for the full width of the net, and secured with tape at the top and bottom. I find that a strip of tape at the centre helps to hold the net correctly as well. Then, every seven or eight paces, secure another stake at top and bottom only, leaving the body of the net free to bag. When you get to the other end of the net, fasten the end stake through the net, and tape top, middle and bottom, like its partner at the beginning. I also find it helpful to have light-coloured masking tape at the top of the two end stakes, so that they may be more easily distinguished from their fellows. Finally, it is useful to catch the top of the net to the draw-cord once with a twist of string halfway between each pair of stakes, which means that, on a very windy night, you are not going to have your net blown taut between the stakes and thus lose the all-important bagging at the bottom.

There are variations on this to suit the individual: some like to catch the net at the top and leave the bottom free, some like taller stakes so that if a concentration of rabbits hits the net at one point, the net will not be pulled so far down, some like to put up a straight set where others favour a shallow half-moon shape. Then there are physical constraints in that a tall person

All set up

with long arms and legs will have less trouble in managing yards of net and bundles of stakes than a short person, and of course the endless examples of ingenuity in kitting out a coat with pockets for stakes and net if carried separately, or a large carrying bag with the stakes on the top and the nets within, if you use the ready-attached stakes method. You may even need some method of carrying rabbits ...

A hundred-yard set can be managed comfortably by one person, remembering that the weight of net and stakes must be carried, and that, on a wet night, the net will become heavier with each set. Many long-netters like to work alone, but there are good arguments for a team of two, or even three, as there is help available if something goes wrong, for instance, somebody injured or taken ill, or the car breaking down, and extra rabbit-carrying power if you have a red-letter night.

Tidiness and attention to detail is vital for setting a long-net; system is all, and it is not a time for sloppiness. The net must be set between the rabbit buries and the place where they are feeding. This is why you want that dark, windy night, because it is all rather pointless if the rabbits hear you and head for home before you have the net set up. If the field has a rise to it, and the rabbits feed over the rise, then you have a good chance of setting your net unnoticed. It is possible to buy a net which can be set with the mesh fastened up, to be dropped by pulling on a remote cord. The idea is that you leave the net ready-staked for a day or two, to get the rabbits used to the change of scenery, then drop the net while they are out. The disadvantages are that you cannot then pick the ideal weather for your night, and that you run the risk of getting your net stolen, vandalised, or even used in your absence! On your own land, or in remote areas where ramblers tend not to roam, it is probably a very useful option.

With a more conventional set, supposing the rabbits are a good way out and oblivious to your presence, you anchor one end of the top net cord with a small peg – a tent-peg is ideal – and then one of you pays out the net, and the other sets the stakes with a half-hitch of the bottom cord around the bottom of each one, and a full hitch of the top cord around the top of each stake by means of half a hitch from each side in turn, keeping the top cord taut and shaking out the bottom of the net so that there is plenty of kill. Two one hundred yard sets, overlapping at the join, are the most usual, and a pair of experienced operators can set these in a matter of minutes. At the end of each net, anchor the top cord again. Some operators work without the anchoring pins, which again is a matter of individual choice; personally I find them useful, though it is something else to carry. Taking up the net is every bit as critical as setting it, for if you do not take up in an orderly manner, you will be faced with spending what seems to be the rest of your life untangling the thing before you can use it again. If one person takes up

LEFT:
Ready to take up

BELOW:
Taking up the net single-handed

Neatly stowed away

stake by stake, stacking the stakes together sideways, the other can straighten the mesh and pick out the debris as you go. And there will be some debris! Not for nothing did the old keepers strew likely long-netting ground with thorn and branchlets; you won't even need an old-style keeper to prove to you that every leaf, twig and piece of detritus will stick to your net as no rabbit ever did. After your rabbiting foray, you will need to stake your net out again at home partly to dry it, and also to mend any tears and pick out the smaller bits and pieces that you missed in the darkness. Each time you fold and pack your net, tie it top and bottom so that it does not sneakily tangle, and will be paid out easily next time you use it. Being a short person, I find a centre tie useful as well.

The clothes you wear while long-netting are important in that you do not want any external buttons or zips for the mesh to catch on, because, believe me, if it can, it will. Make sure that there are no hooks or buckles on your boots as well, and don't wear a watch. The middle of a field on a pitch dark night is not the time to be handcuffed to your net, and will not enhance your credibility with your friends.

Now to the bit you are here for, which is the catching of rabbits. Supposing they are still out there feeding, and quite unsuspecting of your evil machinations – you now need to cause them to run into the net. And they must hit that net running, or they won't be caught, which is why you have not set it too close to the buries themselves, because you know from observation that a rabbit usually pauses before it enters its home. Too close and you will not enmesh the rabbits, too far out and the feeding rabbits will hear you and you will lose the lot. Just in case you were hoping for measurements, the distance varies with the rabbit colony, and your best bet is to chase them in with a dog one evening before you go out, and see how close in they get before they slow down. Remember what Montgomery said: 'Time spent in reconnaissance is never wasted'.

But back to now, with your nets set, and your rabbits feeding quietly. Much has been made of the use of a trained dog for long-netting, and those that are good are very good indeed, but not so easy to find. The dog would need to be taken to the other end of the field, or else sent in a wide outrun, and then would be required to zigzag across the field back towards you, panicking the rabbits to make them run home, but not making any attempt to catch them. The dog, when it reaches the net, must not attempt to catch or pin any rabbit in the net, and must not itself become tangled in it. By the time the dog arrives, you and your colleague if you have one will have your hands full with going along the net necking the rabbits (see page 125), and you won't have time to issue orders to the dog, which must either pull off the pursuit before it reaches the net, or leap the net and then stay out of the way. There is no reward in this for the dog, no catch at the end of the chase, and it is not a discipline that will suit all that many dogs. The most likely long-netting dogs are those with a lot of border collie blood, and not too young, so that the herding instinct has taken over from the chasing instinct.

It is questionable whether a first-class long-netting dog should be exposed to any other rabbiting discipline, for fear of unsteadying it. No doubt all-rounders exist, but they must be as rare as rocking-horse droppings, and you would need to be doing a lot of long-netting to justify keeping a dog for this purpose alone. Daytime long-netting is a little different, and I know quite a few dogs that will chase a rabbit into the net, leap the net and pin the rabbit from the other side without hurting the net or the rabbit. I have had two of my own do this job with virtually no training, so I cannot claim any credit: all I did was show them the net, teach them to jump it and then get them to hold a dead rabbit in the bottom of

Two lurchers covering either side of the net – an unusual sight

the net. The father of my present dog taught himself at the age of nine months on the very first time he was taken ferreting. The first time he chased the rabbit into the net and netted himself as well, though luckily with no damage to net or dog. Bedlingtons and their crosses have a lot of dignity, and he was very put out at having made a fool of himself. The very next rabbit was handled in textbook fashion, pinned in the far side of the net, and fulsome praise ensured that he performed this skill ever after when used with a long-net. A very smart little dog to have worked it out for himself, and I asked his owner that day if I could use the little chap to line my bitch, a decision that I have never regretted.

As the fabled long-netting dog is not available to everybody, a trained human will be a lot easier. Said human need do no more than enter the field at the opposite end to the long-net, and walk in a wide zigzag until he gets to the net and is able to help the person who is, you hope, trying to despatch the huge number of rabbits that have fled into the net. Some recommend shaking a box of matches or tin of pebbles as they walk, or flapping a white kerchief. The old poaching books make much of the use of a device called a 'dead dog' which is a line of rope with a man at either end and which is dragged across the field to rouse the rabbits that are sitting tight. All I can say to that is the rabbits must have sat a devil of a lot tighter in the old days, for my findings are that nowadays the mere fact of a person entering the field is quite enough to send the rabbits pelting for home. And then, curse the little chaps, they don't seem to have read the same books as the would-be long-netter, because they veer away from the net and run out at the sides, or turn back past the matchbox-rattler, or avail themselves of other rabbit-holes away from what you thought was the main bury. They might feed together, they might play together, but they do not necessarily live together.

You must be very quick once rabbits do hit the net, for some will stay still but most struggle like the very devil, and can struggle themselves free just as easily as they can tangle themselves in. Some trapped rabbits will find the time to chew a hole in your net, which will affect any other sets that you had planned that night. Too many rabbits in one spot may bring the net down which tangles that little group but allows others to leap the net to freedom, and you could turn others back just by being there. Kill the rabbits in the net and move to the next ones as fast as possible; once dead they are not going anywhere, nor are they suffering, but you need to run along the net to stop as many rabbits as you can. This is where that second, or even third person can make such a difference, but agree before you start which end of the net you are covering, or you will get in each other's way. Leave the dead rabbits belly-up for collection, so that the white fur makes them easier to see in the dark, and you won't suffer that moment of supreme annoyance that follows accidentally treading on one.

Success

Other things than rabbits can be caught in long-nets at night, and most of them are capable of bringing the whole operation to a halt. Untangling an owl is difficult until you have caught a hedgehog, and those are a piece of cake compared to netting a cat and trying to free it without your net or yourself being shredded; both of you will, of course, be covered in something that carries a lingering stench. Best of all is if brock trundles into your net, because he will just keep walking, taking the net and the stakes with them, tangling everything into a memorable witch's nest and destroying your precious net. You will have to cut him free, there is no other way, and he will not stay still while you are helping him. When you do your pre-netting recce, check for local badger setts, and if there are any, I would suggest that you catch the rabbits by a different method. Equally, do not net a field that has livestock in it, which will approach you out of curiosity or in hope of food, destroy your set and possibly injure themselves, and cause what may be a permanent coolness between you and the landowner. It is important to check your proposed sets the day before, in case stock is moved into the fields that you were intending to work. A telephone call to the landowner is not always enough; sometimes a farmworker will move stock early or later than originally agreed, unaware either that you will be netting, or that the stock is not compatible with the long-netting process.

I was taught long-netting by a rabbiter with a lot of experience of night-netting on the South Downs, where, if you choose your area, there is not a lot of thorn, and the grass is short turf. Even so, he never claimed the huge catches that you read about; there were of course more rabbits about before the myxomatosis, and maybe there was a little exaggeration by the old poachers here and there. This man would set four or five times a night, each time taking up the nets and picking out the debris before going to the next set. He found it marvellous sport, and well worth the trouble. I have found otherwise; most of my rabbiting is in areas that are unsuitable for long-netting because of the assorted bits and pieces that catch in the nets, and also the rabbits here are so spooky that a night set without alerting them is hard to achieve. During the daytime, I have found a stop-net or long-net useful to bisect a hedge or backstop a ditch, or to surround a small patch of rough covert, but the real art of long-netting, while ably demonstrated at shows by those far more experienced than I am, I suspect is a part of the old days, a craft that is vanishing for good reason, and therefore to be enjoyed mostly for its own special reputation. No doubt there are areas of the country where it is still a useful way of catching rabbits, and if you ever get the chance of learning long-netting from a master, do so, for it is a fascinating discipline. While I still use my long-nets a few times a year, it is only by day now, through my own experience and inclination. Long-netting is for the purists, a particular kind of terrain and, to make it worthwhile, where there are unusually high numbers of rabbits. I am conscious that it is my own lack of skill as well as the geography of where I live that has stopped me from getting the most out of my long-nets, and thus I offer no criticism when I describe the drawbacks to their use. Entirely for my own preference, I can find better occupation on dark, windy nights.

A brace caught on the other side

8 TRAPS AND SNARES

*E*ver since we first raised our knuckles off the ground, people have used traps and snares to catch animals. In this country, at this time, there is very little that is legally available to use, and what there is comes under a great deal of criticism from those who do not have any experience of such equipment. There is strong pressure to outlaw all forms of trapping and snaring, which means that those of us who employ these methods of control must take care to be beyond criticism, for if trapping and snaring were to be banned, a major and very efficient method of rabbit control would be lost to us.

Traps and snares are cheap compared to other methods, can operate in a diversity of areas, are long-lasting, need no feeding, training or housing, no certification, little in the way of care and maintenance, and work twenty-four hours a day in any weather. They will do their job while you are getting on with something else, require competence rather than skill, a minimum of attention, and are easily replaced when they wear out. On the other hand, no matter how carefully they are set, there is a slight risk of catching non-target species, and there is a perception of distress caused to the rabbit in those cases where it is confined, though unharmed, until the trapper visits.

Snaring

The snare, more usually called a 'wire' consists of a loop attached to a peg, and is held in place by a stick customarily called a tealer, set-pin or stander, depending on which part of the country you come from. Only free-running snares are legal, which relax when the caught animal stays still and tighten when it struggles: the self-locking snare, which tightened on a moving animal and stayed tight, has now been banned. So once the snared animal accepts the restriction of the snare and stays still, the snare merely holds it, and there is no risk of it slowly being throttled, as there was with the self-locking snare. There are all sorts of variations on the basic design: the country boys of old would plait or twist horsehair, some modern ones use nylon, but brass wire is the most usual, and all that is available if you are buying rather than making your own snares. Two simple modifications to snares are recommended in *Fair Game* (see Bibliography) which are well worth considering: one is to put a kink in the beginning of the noose to keep its size correct, and the other is to put a wire or similar 'stop' creating a minimum diameter on the noose, so that if the wrong animal puts a foot in the snare, it will not be held by it.

The tealer is traditionally hazel-wood, but plain, thick wire will do the job just as well; likewise the peg is traditionally wood, but may be made of metal, though this is heavier to carry. The peg needs to be stout enough to survive repeatedly being knocked into the ground, and long enough not to pull out when the snare catches a rabbit. Wire breaks, string rots, and baler twine isn't half as stout as it used to be, so whatever you use to attach your wire to your peg must be checked every time you take your snare up. The tealer's job is to hold the noose in place, and therefore it does not have to be strong. Some people make their snares so that the tealer is integral with the snare, and others prefer to keep them separate. It is a matter of trying each way and finding the one that suits you best. The loop may be round or pear-shaped, and about the diameter of a man's kneecap. You want the rabbit's head in the noose not its body, and this is worth bearing in mind if you are summer-snaring where there are a lot of half-grown rabbits about. Growing youngsters of any species eat far more than adults, and the amount of damage that juvenile rabbits can do to a growing crop is colossal, so summer

Snare attached to hardwood peg

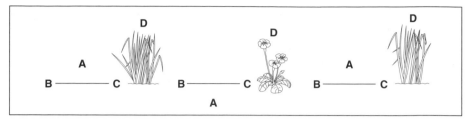

Profile of rabbit run and where to set snare

A   *Set snare here*

B,C   *Flattened ground where rabbit set feet*

D   *Do not set snare here*

snaring along the run lines in arable fields can make an appreciable difference by harvest time.

Where, and to a lesser extent, when you set your snares can make all the difference to your success. Rabbits follow the same runs across fields between their homes and their grazing grounds, and these runs are easily seen. When you look closely, you can see the marks of rabbit fore and hind feet striking the ground in exactly the same spot every time: the grass or crop is flattened in a small spot (forefeet) and a larger spot (hind feet) with grass untouched between. It is very thoughtful of the rabbits to be so consistent, otherwise we would find snaring them much harder. Now picture a hopping rabbit: as its forefeet touch the ground, so its head and neck is extended, and that is what you want in your snare. Therefore set your wire so that the loop is where the forefeet have flattened the grass. The peg is to one side, hammered right into the ground, either straight or at an angle of forty-five degrees. It needs to be flush with the ground surface or otherwise concealed so that the rabbit does not shy sideways away from it and miss the loop. Likewise, the tealer should not stand out as anything more than a thin piece of twig or tarnished wire – no shiny new snares, please, but ones that have been weathered since you bought or made them.

Snaring or trapping, your hands and equipment should be free of scents that would disturb a rabbit, so no cleaning out your ferrets before you set out. Many trappers choose to rub soil through their hands before they commence, and this or a handful of grass will take care of everyday hand smells. How high do you set your snare? Higher than you might at first think. The general idea is about five to five and a half inches, but if rabbits are travelling through long grass, or there is a heavy dew or rain, they will hop higher, and six inches might be better. So let's check that set again: out far enough from the buries so that the rabbit will be travelling freely, along one of the well-used runs, next to where the rabbit's front feet touch the ground, peg out of sight, tealer looking like nothing more than an innocent twig, wire thin and dull enough to be invisible. How will you find it again? Set your snares in lines, and mark the end of each line with a white pebble or a twig set in the ground so that it won't blow over. Count the number of wires you set, for you will not be popular with the farmer if you leave one behind and it catches a sheep by the foot or a calf by the mouth some months later. As with ferreting, never set wires in fields with livestock in, and always warn the landowner when you are coming, and advise when all wires have been taken up. There was a time when I would have recommended that you tell anyone occupying the cottages around the land, so that they can keep their cats in, but nowadays this small courtesy often results in open hostility and stolen snares.

Wires can also be set in fences, where the runs used by rabbits are clearly seen. Just the loop needs to be set, tied around the bottom strand of a barbed wire fence to hang below into the run, but do not do this if there are game birds about, especially pheasants, as you may catch those and be suddenly deeply unpopular with the gamekeeper. The same applies to free-range poultry. If there is stock-fencing, with the large squared mesh, then rabbits tend to leap through the first or second square, depending on how high the surrounding undergrowth is, and so set your wires in the appropriate square. Runs just below the tops of banks are good places to set, too, and with these, the rabbit is likely to break its neck as it hits the snare, which is better for the rabbit as well

It is traditional to set your wires at dusk and check them at daybreak, but rabbits move around during the day as well, and if you live close enough to your set to be able to check it during the day, then if you re-set after the first catch, you should get more rabbits. After that, they will smell and see the disruption caused by the capture of their fellows, and you will do no further good there. Also, if the area that you are working is open to human traffic, you are probably better to pick up at daybreak and set again at dusk, for the presence of people equals vandalism and stolen snares, plus certain types may seek a confrontation and keep returning, thus spoiling other methods of control and presenting risk and nuisance when you wish to shoot.

All sorts of beings have an interest in your snares when they catch, and you will find rabbit heads but no rabbit, which is the work of a fox or dog, rabbits eaten from underneath, which means that the badger got there first, or rabbits eaten messily along the back fillet, which is a cat's contribution to your worries. The badger eats what he needs, the fox will take several carcases, but the cat will spoil more. Do not feed these to your ferrets, for cats have a variety of diseases that they can pass on to ferrets and which are likely to kill them. Crows and magpies will peck the eyes out of snared rabbits, which is another reason to get to your catch at daybreak, before they can do this. It doesn't spoil the meat, but is a dreadful thing for the rabbit to suffer. A dog that gets the habit of raiding snares is a tremendous nuisance, as it will follow your scent and find your wires all over the farm. One of my lurchers was a great finder of illegally-set wires, and brought me many headless rabbits to hand while we were out exercising, which amused the gamekeeper no end.

If snares are properly set, there is only a small risk of catching things other than rabbits, but it does happen. Pheasants and cats, occasionally very small terriers, may be caught, and cats are certainly the most difficult to release without sustaining damage to yourself. Don't use your bare hands, but loosen the wire with care using a claw hammer or similar hooked instrument, and don't get your legs too near, either. Pussy will leave the snare and surrounding area smelling atrocious, and there will be no profit in setting a snare there for quite some days, unless it rains. Don't put that snare with your others when you are taking up, but keep it separate until it has aired.

Be methodical when you are taking up, count your snares in as you have counted them out, and straighten out any kinks in the wire if you are re-setting, making sure that the noose runs freely. Remember that brass wire becomes brittle after stress, and will break after it has made a few catches, especially if a rabbit has been lively. When you go to take up, you will find that many of your rabbits are dead, but some will still be alive and will try to get away from you as you approach. To minimise their stress, stand on the wire to hold them and then despatch them still in the snare, before you release them. If for any reason you need to release a rabbit alive, for instance if it is one of the black ones that you have been asked not to kill, hold it by the loose skin atop the back, where it cannot kick you as is struggles, while you loosen the wire. Go along your line despatching the rabbits first, and then return picking up the snares and bodies. This is more humane for the rabbits. Capably done, snaring will make big inroads into a rabbit infestation, the carcases are clean and saleable, and once you get your confidence, you will be able to set and take up quickly. It is a feature of the age we live in that snaring has to be so much more discreetly done nowadays, but then the poachers of old had to be discreet as well. Better that than to lose this most valuable method of rabbit control due to the interference of those who don't understand where their food comes from.

Trapping

There are three forms of trapping rabbits that are legal today: the spring trap, the box or multicatch trap and the cage trap. Several forms of spring trap are legal, as set out in the Spring Trap Approval Orders 1995 though

Fenn Vermin VI rabbit trap, still manufactured, shown set and ...

... shown sprung

Single spring Imbra: legal but no longer made. Shown set

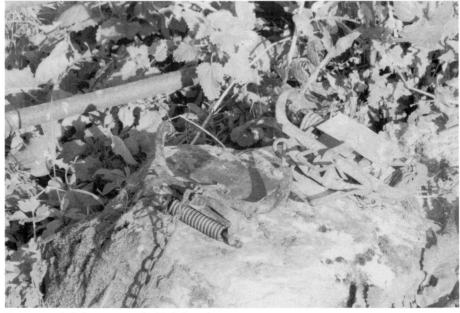

FRONT: *single Imbra*, (REAR): *double Imbra, shown set*

Single and double Imbra shown sprung

only the Fenn Rabbit, Fenn Vermin VI and Springer 6 and the Magnum Bodygrip are still manufactured. The Juby and Imbra are no longer made, but still very much in use, and are legal. These traps must be set right into the rabbit burrow, not in the entrance where they may trap birds dusting in the soft soil excavated by the rabbits. As well as your traps, you will need a container of sieved soil that is free from small stones and twigs that would foul their operation: some people diligently collect suitable soil whenever they see it, from molehills and rabbit bury entrances, and others sieve the soil as they go along. A tealer or setting stick, a trapping hammer and a trowel or similar for scraping out the trap bed will complete your equipment.

First of all, you need to scrape a bed for the trap inside the burrow, remembering that a rabbit will not hop into a dip but over it, so once set, the surface of the trap must be flush with the level of the burrow floor, or slightly higher, but not lower. The trap must be set sufficiently deeply for the arms to swing upwards and not catch on the tunnel roof when the trap is sprung in the case of the Imbra and Fenn. The Bodygrip operates differently, with the arms of the trap swinging forwards, and so the area in front of the trap should be free as well, to allow it to work. Next, fix the peg firmly into the ground and flush with it, for which a hammer will be necessary. Set your trap and place it into the bed that you have created for it, using the tealer or

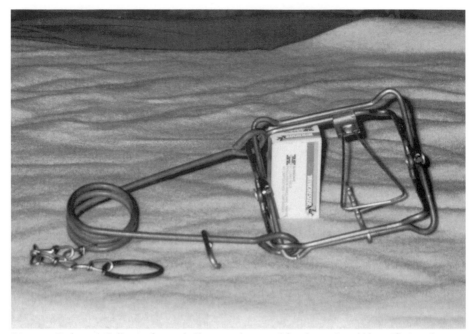

Magnum Bodygrip. Still manufactured. Shown set but raised for clarity (would be set flat) and …

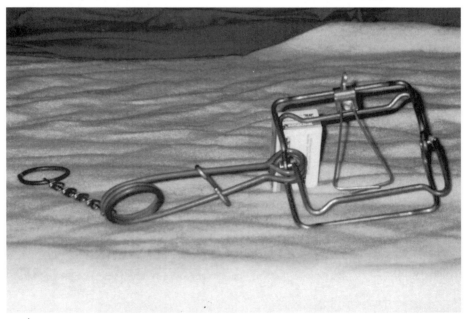

… shown sprung

Multicatch drop trap shown in two separate parts ... shown assembled with trapdoor closed ...

... with trapdoor raised. When set, only tunnel is above ground

setting stick to manoeuvre it and then take off the safety catch. Last of all, scatter a thin layer of the sieved soil over the whole trap, chain, peg, everything, so that the floor of the burrow is level, and nothing shows through. With a little practice, you will soon be able to set traps quickly and neatly. These traps can also be set legally in an artificial tunnel outside a rabbit bury, along an established run under a fence, for instance, but under no circumstances may they be set in the open. When checking your traps, spring any unsprung ones with your tealer before drawing them out using your hammer. These traps almost always kill, but on occasion do not, so it is very important to visit your traps at least once, and preferably twice, every twenty-four hours. The Bodygrip trap is particularly efficient, and rarely fails to kill, but even so, traplines should be visited as recommended.

Live Catch Traps

Cage Traps
These are made of wire or wood and wire, and are legal to use in the open. They operate on a treadle plate system, and there are several designs. Particularly useful with garden rabbit problems where shooting is not possible and the buries are away from the affected land, these traps are most usually baited with sliced carrot, though I understand that salt or sugar is

Live trap set in garden

Baited trap, rabbit's eye view

also very effective. I have also heard of vanilla essence being used – be sparing! – and also peppermint, aniseed and fresh parsley, but I have no personal experience of the success or otherwise of these last. Care must be taken to secure them firmly, as with some designs, if the rabbit can tip the cage over, the door can fall open. Rabbits confined in cage traps are safe from the attentions of crows and the like, but are very frightened at their confinement, and so as much diligence is required with checking live-traps as with any other sort. The stink of scared rabbit really clings to these traps, and so they cannot be re-used until this has been dispersed.

Box Traps or Drop Traps
These are usually wooden or wood and metal, and there are no legal restrictions on their size. They are positioned along rabbit runs against fences or walls, and can also be used with success in overgrown woodland. Rabbits like an easy life as much as we do, and if a narrow path is cleared along a regular route from buries to feeding grounds through fallen woodland debris, they will take the path in preference to negotiating the brash. Once they are using the path well, the trap is set flush with the ground. The deeper the trap, the more rabbits it will hold; the bottom of the

trap must be wired in to prevent escapes, and these traps must be visited and emptied frequently. It requires a certain amount of care to extract the rabbits without either being bitten, or getting an escapee full in the face as it makes a bid for freedom. Another drawback, particularly in winter, is the frequency with which you catch hedgehogs; getting these out is quite a challenge, and remember that a hedgehog bite is a dirty bite, and must be treated as soon as possible, as otherwise it will fester.

I make no apology for stressing one more time that if you set snares or traps, it is incumbent upon you to check these very frequently. Likewise, if you are setting live-traps, it is important to despatch the rabbits as soon after you take them out of the trap as you can. This can occasionally pose problems if your landowner (usually the garden-rabbit sufferer) insists that the rabbits are not killed but released somewhere else; not a very moral stance as they then become a nuisance to someone different, and meantime undergo unnecessary stress through being confined in a vehicle. There is no reasoning with this sort of person, and so it is best just to go along with his or her wishes and remove the rabbits to despatch them as soon as possible afterwards, though I knew someone years ago who would release them on the edge of the neighbouring land, knowing that they would soon be home. Surprisingly, it is not illegal to re-release pest species somewhere else, unless they are recent introductions such as grey squirrels or mink. Having been here for a thousand years or more, rabbits seem to be exempt.

A morning's catch

There will be occasions when people ask you to provide them with live rabbits. Please do not: the purposes for which they require them are likely to be inhumane and possibly illegal. If someone wants a rabbit for a pet, there are plenty of domestic rabbits bred from generations of tame stock that are very happy to be living with and handled by humans; wild rabbits are a different matter entirely.

Every trapper has different little tricks and wrinkles for setting or improving on the standard trap or snare, bits of this or that made in the workshop, small changes to the original design, and if you get the chance to go out with an experienced trapper, take it, for some of these improvements will be useful to you. Just as each different environment poses its own challenges, so the human predator will rise to the occasion. Several useful and informative videos and DVDs have been made, and at the time of writing I can recommend those by Glen Waters, *The Warrener*, and Moucher Productions; no doubt there will be others before long. Readers can find videos advertised regularly in *Countryman's Weekly*. However, nothing can match going out and setting your own traps and snares, and you will be agreeably surprised at how straightforward it is, and how effective, following the guidelines set out above.

Caught!

9 GAS, FENCING AND REPELLENTS

These methods are all by far the most expensive but nonetheless should be covered in this book.

Gas

The use of gas should be considered a last resort, and every other alternative should be tried first. Professional pest controllers frequently have to deal with customers who would like gas to be used without considering other options, but their own training emphasises that any other method is preferable to the use of gas. The gas is an indiscriminate killer, and there is no stopping it once it is launched – it just goes on killing whatever is in its path. It is expensive if used properly, and will only hold the problem at bay for a year or so, less if there is a significant population of rabbits living above ground. Strangely enough, it is often the first choice for the squeamish, because, like rat poison, the killing is unseen.

Two types of gas used to be available: Cymag (hydrogen cyanide, HCN) which comes in powder form, and Phostoxin (phosphine, PHC). Both types of material generate gas upon contact with moist air: the normal humidity of air in this country is quite sufficient to cause this reaction, and therefore extreme caution must be exercised at all times when gas is in use. Due to increased regulatory requirements, Cymag was withdrawn from use in UK in December 2004, leaving only the hydrogen phosphide options of Phostoxin and Talunex, which each come in pellet or tablet form. These substances are licensed for use on rabbits and rodents only; it must be stressed that their use on any other species is illegal.

Many pest controllers regret the loss of Cymag which, while slightly more difficult to apply, was considered more versatile and effective, especially for larger warrens, but such is progress.

Strict regulations cover the use of gas, with which operators should be up to date. Storage should be correct, and lids should be replaced on containers

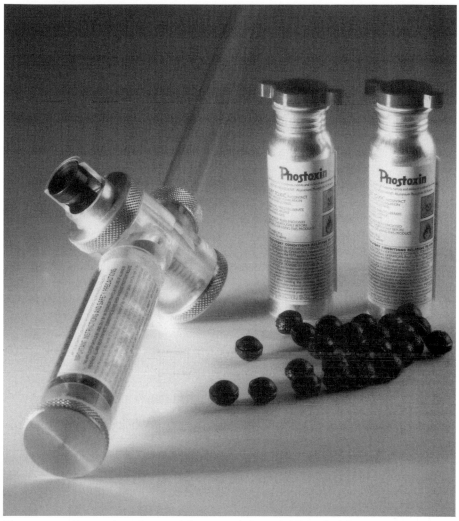

Phostoxin pellets and applicator (photograph Rentokil Initial plc)

immediately that sufficient of the compound has been extracted. Gas should not be transported in the cab of a vehicle, and should be carried in such a manner that spillage is impossible. If it is to be carried on commercial transport, appropriate clearances may need to be obtained in advance of the journey.

Although for best results gassing should be carried out in winter, the use of gas is unwise on wet or windy days, or in conditions of high humidity. It should never be used in proximity to buildings of any sort, because it is impossible to govern where the gas will emerge once it is underground. It must not be used near ponds, rivers or other water courses, or near areas accessible to children or livestock. The operator should be careful not to get chemical on clothing or skin, to cover any open cuts, and of course must not smoke. Gas should never be used by someone operating alone, and the antidote should always be carried. Both operators should be familiar with the use of the antidote, which is amyl nitrate. The capsule should be broken under the nose of the victim so that it may be inhaled, and professional medical assistance should be sought immediately. It is recommended to carry a kelocyanor antidote pack, but this should only be used by a doctor. If the victim has stopped breathing, DO NOT use mouth-to-mouth resuscitation; instead, artificially respirate using chest massage. There is no chance to help yourself if you are accidentally gassed: the merest whiff will render you insensible, and people have been killed while gassing through not taking adequate safety precautions.

The buries should be cleared to expose each hole prior to gassing, and surrounding areas of undergrowth driven out with a dog prior to commencement, so that as many rabbits as possible are to ground. The dog must then be confined well away from the operating area. Insert the gas pellets using the applicator according to the manufacturer's instructions. The hole is then immediately sealed with a plug of turf, grass side downwards. A lethal concentration of gas is released at once, building up about 2ft (0.6m) from the bury entrance, and persisting for around twenty-four hours.

The job is not complete until the buries have been re-visited forty-eight hours later, and any holes that have been opened up should then be gassed and blocked as before. Then the bury should remain unused for a year or so, as the presence of so much death underground will deter other rabbits from moving in.

With the gas inserted and the holes blocked, death is quick for the rabbits, and for anything else which happens to be living down the rabbit holes, such as little owls, hedgehogs, snakes, or even the odd cat. There is no way to avoid gassing non-target species, which is one reason why the use of gas is so controversial.

Fencing

Rabbit-proof fencing is equally controversial on welfare grounds, though the reason for this may not be immediately obvious. Rabbits fenced in or out of an area without other means of control being initiated suffer the effects of overcrowding: disease, starvation and stress. This will certainly kill them, but sufficiently slowly to allow them to breed, so while little

A properly erected rabbit fence

overall reduction in numbers may be observed, the rabbits will be in poor health and considerable distress. If, however, rabbit fencing is used in conjunction with active steps being taken to reduce the surrounding rabbit population, it can be both humane and effective. It is an extremely expensive option, and is therefore normally used to protect relatively small areas, such as gardens or allotments. I have seen attempts to reduce crop damage by fencing one side of a field, but the rabbits simply found the end of the fence and went round it. However, the existence of the fence certainly shortened the odds in favour of the dog when a dog was used to catch these rabbits as the dog would either pin the rabbits against the fence, or run to the end of the fence ahead of the rabbits, turn, and let them run into her mouth. If rabbit fencing is to be used, then the whole of the area to be protected must be enclosed, otherwise the entire exercise is a waste of time, labour and money.

Rabbits are proficient at jumping and digging which, while it may seem blindingly obvious, seems to be disregarded with some forms of rabbit fencing that I have seen. It is no good doing this on the cheap, because in order to be effective, the bottom of the fence must be dug in at an angle towards the outside of the fence and deeply enough to deter burrowing. It must also be high enough that rabbits cannot easily jump it – remember that

Rabbit fence broached by rabbits – note hole in foreground

Showing what happens if the fence is not buried correctly

they will have plenty of incentive to want to do so. The fencing itself must be sufficiently robust to survive several years of local climate, usually ten-gauge wire netting with hexagonal mesh. Special straining equipment is necessary for installation. Subsequent maintenance is minimal, though undergrowth should not be permitted to grow up close to the fence, where it will provide a useful foothold for ambitious rabbits, and tree roots will push through it. Fencing will last longer if it is away from stray human traffic; there are some people who cannot see a static method of pest control without damaging it.

Electric Fencing

Electric fencing can be extremely useful in rabbit deterrence, either the portable netting kind used on a temporary basis until a crop has outgrown the vulnerable stage, or as an adjunct to permanent rabbit fencing in the shape of a single wire approximately 5in (2cm) above ground level, to dissuade the rabbits from digging. Ground cover must be kept down by mowing or spraying, to prevent the unit shorting, and this will have to be repeated frequently during the growing season. The fence should be attached to the electrical supply through a high-powered fence control unit, which must be attached to a metallic earthing rod that is driven almost completely into the soil as near to the centre of the fence as practicable, in order to secure maximum voltage over the longest distance. Unfortunately, such fencing is also vulnerable to theft and vandalism, and in certain areas may not be a suitable option for this reason.

Trees

Tree guards are a necessity when growing saplings in rabbit country, and there are several sorts commercially available, from plastic sleeves, tubes or netting, to welded wire mesh. Various scent-repellents are also available, the best-known of which is Renardine, readily available from farm suppliers. With repellents, care should be taken to follow the directions precisely, as some makes can be damaging to plant life. For the gardener, various exotic remedies have been cited from time to time, such as lion dung (now commercially available), human hair clippings from hairdressers, or the cleanings from ferret hutches. You might, on reflection, prefer to put up with the rabbits. Scent deterrents will only last until heavy rain puts an end to their efficacy, and so need frequent renewal.

Stinking Out

This delightful term refers to the practice of putting foul-smelling substances down rabbit holes with the intention of keeping the rabbits above ground so that they may be shot. This will only work for a very short time, and is unlikely to put off a rabbit that is heading for home, having perceived that it is in danger. If you want to try this, please steer clear of environmentally unfriendly substances – in my childhood, Jeyes' Fluid, creosote or paraffin were commonly used. Specially manufactured repellents are available, or else you can make your own. Most warreners have a vile and secret recipe of their own that is biodegradable, but probably not as quickly as you would wish if you happen to spill any on yourself. The system is to soak old newspapers or rags in the substance and then shovel them down the rabbit holes. I did hear of potatoes being rolled in the hell-brew and then pushed down the holes, which my Mother would have called a shocking waste of food.

Rabbits that are underground when stinking-out commences will leave their homes to lie above ground as long as the buries are fairly small. If rabbit holes have to be filled in, for instance on racehorse gallops, it is a good idea to use a repellent down the holes first, but unless the rabbits are killed by some other means at the same time, new holes will appear very soon. While we are on the subject of putting things down rabbit holes, some people have success by blocking the rabbit holes a rabbit length inside the entrance, the idea being that when the rabbits run home, they will sit as far inside the rabbit hole as they can get, and then they can be pulled out by hand. Holes need to be solidly blocked if you want to follow this method; although I have read of rabbits being fooled by crumpled paper or a plastic sack, my own experience is that they batter down whatever barrier they can shift, or else dash out again, though that might be sufficient to allow a dog to catch them. It can be useful if you are ferreting to block adjacent buries with this in mind, if you are short of nets, although nets are easier to carry, and backnetting is every bit as successful.

Garden rabbits

One problem that you will often be asked to help with is that of wild rabbits coming into gardens. Usually, the garden backs onto woodland or arable land, which is where the rabbits are living, and it is difficult to deal with rabbits unless you can get at their homes. The owner of the garden is usually unaware of the fact that he is running the breakfast part of a bed-and-breakfast service, and thinks that the rabbits are living in the garden.

Although the neighbouring landowner(s) have a legal 'Duty of Care' under the 1954 Pests Act to deal with the rabbits, neighbours have to be lived with, and your customer may prefer not to tackle them. Very occasionally you can get permission from the neighbours to enter their land for rabbit control purposes, but mostly they are unwilling. Often there is someone who 'likes to see the rabbits about', and I have more than once been smuggled in to deal with the rabbits when this person is away!

Sometimes the garden owner has provided good rabbit habitat in the form of seasoning wood, bonfires or overgrown areas. Under the garden shed is a good place for rabbits to set up home, and not the easiest for getting the ferret out, should she lie-up. By the time the rabbit-holes appear in the garden, there can be sizeable earthworks under the shed; often the owners will block up the rabbit holes and be most indignant when others appear! Keen gardeners feel faint at the prospect of their lawns being dug up by keen ferreters, and a rabbit caught by your dog will not be sufficient compensation for the dog ploughing through a flowerbed to do it. Thus for gardens, I generally recommend restricting rabbit access from outside, preferably with rabbit fencing, removal of rabbit-friendly areas within, and live-traps. If the garden-owner is reasonably laid-back about small areas of damage, tacking-in three sides of the shed with chicken-wire, netting the fourth, and putting a ferret in can be successful, as long as you can be good-humoured about a lie-up, and a dog is good value in hunting-out areas of rough, or standing by as the woodpile is taken down. But many garden-owners will not find this acceptable. Most people can tolerate the concept of live-trapping, which is covered in Chapter 8, but you may have to assure them that you are taking bunny away to let him go 'into the wild'. My freezer can get pretty wild at times.

As control methods, gassing, fencing and repellents are at their most effective when used in conjunction with other ways. It is little use trying to keep rabbits out of an area unless the population is reduced at the same time, though this is not always possible when stretches of rabbit-infested land are broken up into small acreages of different ownership. Gassing initially shows dramatic results, but if there is a high rabbit population, then other rabbits will move into the gassed area to eat, even if not to live, so the damage will only be reduced temporarily. Hungry rabbits will eventually broach the most efficient fencing, and in our climate, repellents will need to be refreshed very frequently. However, if these methods are used to underpin a continuous rabbit control programme, they will prove well worth while.

10 FROM FIELD TO TABLE

*F*irst catch your rabbit! And then, having caught it, what next?
Rabbits are good, healthy, free-range food, more or less organic (they will keep off a sprayed crop if they have alternative food sources, until rain has neutralised the chemical) low in fat and free from additives. They are food for us and our animals, and while the primary reason for rabbiting is pest control, the by-product of fine meat from an impeccable source should not be wasted. Yet we import huge quantities of intensively-reared rabbit while healthy wild rabbits are often difficult to sell. At the time of writing, I can sell all the rabbits I get to our local butcher, but with a large family of dogs, ferrets and the odd human to feed, a lot of the catch is used at home. Some of our village pensioners, who remember when rabbit was a feast, like to have a rabbit now and then, but most people expect it to be delivered oven-ready these days. If you know any snake or hawk owners, these will be glad of a source of wild rabbit, and the snakes don't even require their rabbits paunched. Butchers that will buy wild rabbits, are worth looking after, especially if they will take them paunched and in the skin. However, at Christmas time, butchers' freezers are full of more luxurious fare, and they may not want your rabbits just at the time when you are clearing large quantities of them. Our household now has four freezers, and it is not uncommon for two and a half of them to be full right up with rabbits. I have in the past offered rabbits to various animal rescue groups, but my own experience is that they cannot be bothered with them and would rather feed their animals on cheap manufactured food. The same thing applies with homes for the elderly – the residents would love to eat rabbit, but preparing it is often too much trouble for the cook. Yet it is not difficult, and this is what you do.

If you snare or ferret your rabbits, or have a soft-mouthed dog, you will have to learn how to kill them yourself. There are several ways of doing this. The rabbit punch is a cliché, and not a good way of killing rabbits unless you are very strong, though it is probably the way that everyone has heard

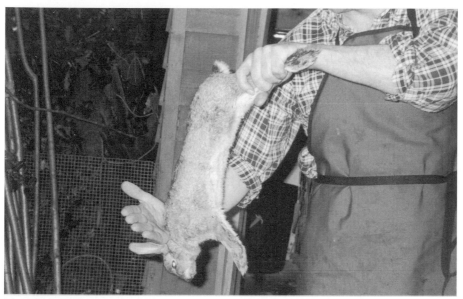

The rabbit punch

One method of chinning

Most usual killing method

The easiest way – grasp rabbit in front of ears and behind eyes, and bend neck upwards

about. It refers to holding the rabbit up by its hindlegs and striking the back of its neck hard with the side of the other hand in a chopping movement. This can bruise the meat and hurt your hand; it can also stun the rabbit rather than killing it, which is inhumane when you consider what happens next. Some buck rabbits have incredibly powerful necks, and it would take an exceptional blow to kill in this manner. There are easier ways. One is to use a 'priest' like anglers do, striking the rabbit on the back of the head with a specially weighted stick or other heavy object. Some people 'chin' the rabbit by holding the knuckles of one hand against the back of the neck where it joins the skull, and pushing down on this while pushing up sharply under its chin with the other hand. This causes a 'hangman's fracture' by breaking the pin of bone that connects the neck to the head. It is a knack that, once mastered, is probably the best way of killing a rabbit that is still in the net. Concentrate, though, because it affords the rabbit the chance to bite you if you are careless with the chin hand. If you are running the length of a long-net despatching rabbits as fast as you can, a moment of inattention can leave you with one hand sufficiently badly bitten to hamper you for the rest of the night and a couple of days afterwards. Does this sound like the voice of experience? It certainly is!

Another very popular method is to take both hindlegs of the rabbit in one hand, clasp the other hand round the neck with your thumb and fingers meeting under the rabbit's chin and pull smartly upwards with the hindleg hand at the same time as pushing the back of the rabbit's head down and lifting its chin with the other. A hangman's fracture again is the result, but you need to be fairly strong in the hand, especially with a burly buck. If you are a small person or have a short wingspan, you can bend the rabbit across your knee for added leverage. The easiest way, and the way I use all the time, is to hold the hindlegs as before, but place the other hand over the rabbit's brow, in front of the ears and behind the eyes. Brace the hindleg hand, and the lightest of flicks with the head hand is sufficient to break the neck. You can kill a lot more rabbits this way before your hands start to cramp up, and it is an ideal method for those with small hands or a less strong grip. Some people prefer to hold the rabbit across the back rather than by the hindlegs, which means that you don't have to cope with what is sometimes vigorous kicking, but you do need a large hand for this, and I prefer to catch hold of the hindlegs. I have also seen rabbits killed by holding them by the head and flicking the body like a whipcrack, which is just as effective, if a little more flamboyant, than the other methods, and also a good way of giving the rabbit a chance to bite you again. There will be times when you need to kill a rabbit as unobtrusively as possible, and this is not the way. Last year, we were exercising the dogs along a local beauty spot when an elderly lady stopped to pass the time of day, and after a few minutes, I realised that one of my lurchers had pinned a rabbit in a large bramble patch behind us. While the Sahib, who knew exactly what had happened, continued to chat, I had to extract, despatch and pocket the rabbit (even on the hottest summer's day, a lurcher owner will be wearing something with deep pockets) as discreetly as I could. Unfortunately I was not able to drain it, so as it relaxed, it piddled posthumously in my pocket, which did not improve my tissues and packet of mints.

Draining the rabbit is indeed what comes next, as soon as you have killed it. Real death is not like the way it is portrayed on the television, as nervous spasm can make a dead rabbit kick and jerk for some seconds, especially if there is a lot of adrenaline in its system from being chased by dog or ferret. Be careful it does not kick or bite you during this time, especially bite, as the jaws will tighten with the muscle spasms and be quite difficult to open, despite your being such a big strong human. Head-shot rabbits will kick and bounce amazingly, which gives rise to the assumption by anti-hunters that these rabbits are wounded and suffering. They are not: they are quite dead. But you can see how the misunderstanding can arise, and as we must be above reproach in all we do when involved in pest control, it is worth taking time to explain to such people and setting their minds at rest – if you can. Our local paper frequently carries accusations of rabbiters being cruel, clearly from those who do not appreciate that death throes come after death not before it, and it is beneficial for pest control as a whole if such letters are answered politely and with a proper explanation. Death is the last taboo in our society, and the killing of animals for whatever reason attracts a lot of misconception. If you are in any doubt about whether a rabbit is dead or not, check the blink reflex by touching its eyeball.

Unless the rabbit was very frightened at the time of its death, in which case it will have drained itself, it will be full of urine, which will taint the meat and fill your pocket or gamebag if left in situ. Draining is best done immediately, before the carcase has had time to stiffen. Hold the rabbit head up and tummy out (check the wind direction) then place a thumb over the centre of its abdomen and draw that thumb smoothly downwards, pressing firmly inwards at the same time. A stream of urine will be expelled. Mind your boots. This should be done as soon after the rabbit is dead as possible, but if rigor mortis has already set in, you will have to wait until the muscles relax again before you can do this job. Times vary: some rabbits go rigid almost immediately, and some can take quite a while. Usually the ones that go straight into rigor mortis are the ones that take longest to wear off again; I believe that it is all to do with adrenaline, which of course varies with the circumstances and the individual.

Having drained your rabbit, or 'peed it out' you may want to hock it for ease of carrying. This is done by inserting the tip of your knife into the

Draining out urine　　　　　　　　　　*Hocked and hung*

hindleg through the membrane between the (Achilles) tendon, or
hamstring, and the flesh. You then push the foot of the other hindleg
through the gap, pull until the hock is through, and you have a handle to
carry your rabbit by, or to thread a stick through and carry on the stick.
Some people don't like to hock their catch because you may have to cut
into the hindleg flesh a little, especially if your rabbit is an adolescent with
big feet and skinny legs. If that is the case, you will need a gamebag, but it
is best not to put rabbits higgledy-piggledy into a gamebag if you are
intending them for sale, as they may come out twisted up and damaged.
The rabbits must cool before they are packed, either by laying them out on
the ground, or hanging them in trees or on fences. The traditional way is
hocked and hung in pairs, belly out to cool the viscera and also be more
visible for when you return to collect them. Rabbits left to cool may be
taken by stray dogs, foxes, cats, badgers, and anything else that finds a
rabbit meal tastier for something else having caught it; I have had two-
legged foxes filch my rabbits as well. Most annoying was some rabbits hung
in a tree that a pair of crows made a fine feast of, leaving not very much
that was useable. I have had a stoat drag off a rabbit almost in front of me,

and I let him have it for his cheek; I have also taken rabbits killed by stoats – a nice clean kill with a bite to the back of the head – so it was only right to return the favour. Generally, rabbits hung in trees are less likely to be taken than those left on the ground, but, like all aspects of working within the natural world, you must reckon to leave something for the other fella from time to time.

Your rabbits are drained and cooled, you have finished your rabbiting, and now you must take them home, paunch (gut) and skin them. There are many ways to paunch rabbits, and however many I tell you about, there will be a few more, so I will cover the most usual methods. You will need your knife as sharp as you can get it.

Holding the rabbit head up and belly out, pick up a fold of belly skin below the ribs and above the genitals and slice it off lengthwise. Put your fingers in the gap and gently pull the skin towards the sides, which will open up as big a hole as you want. In the old days, it was the fashion to have the gap just large enough to insert a finger and thumb, because it was thought to look neater, but nowadays we favour as large an opening as possible, in order to be sure that everything we don't want has been extracted, and to allow for more rapid cooling of the carcase. The membrane holding in the viscera is intact at this point, and it is an easy matter to insert the tip of the knife and make a tiny vertical nick which you then open out with your fingertips. The important thing is to avoid puncturing the guts, but if the rabbits have been shot, or caught by a hard-mouthed dog, this may have happened already, in which case you just make the best of it. Assuming everything is whole, give a tiny shake to the rabbit, which will send everything down into the abdominal cavity, and then look for the liver and stomach which will be high under the top of the ribcage. With the tip of your knife, very carefully detach the stomach from the body by cutting the tube at the top, and then separate the liver from the stomach without piercing the gallbladder – it is better to lose a little piece of liver than cut the gallbladder, which taints the meat. The idea is to retain the liver and free the stomach without covering yourself in its contents. The whole parcel of guts is now loose except for attachment at the other end, which again you cut through at the tube.

The stomach may be full of greenstuff, or, if the rabbit has been underground for a while, may be empty. If the stomach is very full, it is difficult to remove without piercing, and if your rabbits have lain some time, particularly in bitter cold, windy conditions, the guts may have expanded with the stomach gases fermenting, and be rather delicate. If you split them, it cannot be helped and you will not be the first person to have done it, so just mutter an appropriate expletive, wipe the slime off your face and hands and remember to close your mouth next time. Now look at the liver. Is it clean, a healthy colour and a good size, or is it discoloured, speckled with coccidiosis, swollen or shrunken? Check the guts for tapeworm, and if there is one, do not touch it. This will decide whether your rabbit is human or animal food, so cut off the tip of an ear to mark it if you wish, for one or the other.

Look at the kidneys: do they look healthy? Rabbit kidneys are offset as is usual with herbivores. Carnivore kidneys are level, and in the old days, people buying a cleaned rabbit would ask for the kidneys to be left in, not only as a delicacy for eating, but to prove that what you had sold them was a rabbit and not a cat. If your rabbit is a pregnant doe, the young will be arranged in the uterine horns and lying along either side of the rabbit, rather than carried in the front as we do. This is so that even a pregnant rabbit can run for its life if it needs to, without being inconvenienced by the pregnancy. As a doe rabbit spends almost all of her adult life pregnant, this is a very necessary adaptation. While you will not be wanting to eat unborn rabbits, they are a great delicacy for ferrets, so bring along a container and save these for them. A lactating doe will show milk all along the length of her belly, and although such rabbits are perfectly edible, you will find them unsaleable. The dogs and ferrets will enjoy them, however.

Another way to paunch the rabbit is to open it fur and membrane in one go, in one long vertical slit, hold by the back and shake the guts out, and then cut through the tubes fore and aft. I have seen rabbits pulled so far open that the backs have broken; apart from being unnecessarily messy, you break their ribs as well, which makes them difficult to deal with as anything other than ferret food. If a broken bone pierces your skin, the wound, though small, is likely to fester, so take time to treat it accordingly when you get home. Some people like to turn and sling out the guts with a flick of the wrist; this is a knack and a good way to lose friends if you do not check the wind direction first. The advantage is that your hands stay cleaner, and the disadvantage is that the viscera fly you know not where, which can make you very unpopular, and also that you lose the liver. Rabbit guts possess the most clinging pungency, which will retain its hold through all manner of cleaning agents including carbolic soap. I carry a container of baby-wipes so at least my steering wheel does not get the full impact, but find that eau de bunnyguts will cling to me for hours. I am told that tomato juice or tomato ketchup is good for removing strong biological smells, so I may give that a try. Meanwhile, you can guarantee popularity with all dogs and even the most aloof of cats, until the worst of the smell wears off. I know someone who wears surgical gloves for this job, which certainly makes a difference, so if you do find the job too messy and smelly for your tastes, you could try that.

It goes without saying that you uncollar and put away your ferrets before you start paunching your rabbits! You might wish to paunch them on-site, to reduce the carrying weight, in which case please, if you want to stay on good terms with the landowner, dispose of the waste responsibly. Guts are not everybody's favourite sight, especially when vomited up onto the kitchen floor by the farm dog which has been mooching after you and getting in the way all day before feasting on your leavings. I know of more than one ferreter who lost his permission because the farmer's wife got so brassed off with clearing up second-hand guts. So, if you are leaving the paunch on-site, dig a deep hole and bury it properly, and as far from the farmhouse as you can. The foxes will probably disinter and eat it the same night, but they don't yodel it up in the house afterwards, and once it is gone, it is gone.

There are other useful things you can do with rabbit paunch: ducks are crazy about it, as one of my northern friends says in his lovely accent, 'Dooks loov goots'. If you are looking after a flight pond, the quackers will really appreciate a rabbit paunch dinner. Tame ducks love it, too, and most chickens will dispose of rabbit paunch in moments, squabbling over the best bits. Don't donate your bounty to commercial flocks, though, because it is illegal to feed them on this, just as it is illegal to give it to pigs, which would love it. In fact, pigs will eat rabbits, too, given the chance, but the law denies these omnivores meat in their diet, except for whatever a lucky free-ranger might snaffle up with no-one any the wiser. This law is sensible in that disease may be spread otherwise, for instance, a nasty outbreak of swine fever in 2000 was traced back to a ham sandwich given by a rambler to a pig. Some folks give rabbit paunch to their ferrets, but I would not; it is a poor thank-you for all the work they do for you not to give them some decent meat still with the fur or feathers on. Still, in the old days when most ferrets were kept on bread and milk, I suppose even rabbit paunch was well received, and at least gave them some goodness in their wretched diet.

If you are baiting fox traps, or salting (baiting) ground preparatory to lamping foxes, rabbit paunch can be very useful; some foxes like it fresh and others favour carrion, so it can last you for a while. Don't throw your rabbit paunch into water, whatever you do, unless there are 'dooks' ready to receive it because it pollutes the water, and it floats, thus advertising your lack of consideration to the whole world. Your own lake on your own land might be a different matter, if there are fish that might appreciate it, but paunch is better given a decent burial, or fed to something that will enjoy it without legal repercussions. Though I do know of someone who leaves rabbit paunch freely on his estate to encourage dog-walkers to keep to the footpaths and keep their dogs under control, and he maintains that it works better than any amount of notices and polite requests. Now, as the notices in washrooms say, wash your hands! And wash them, and wash them...

When your rabbits are home, divide them into human and animal food, and hang them up where air can circulate freely until you have time to deal with them. Some people like to wedge the paunching gap open with a stick inserted horizontally, to keep the carcase fresh. It is traditional to hang hares head upwards and rabbits head down, but rabbit is not a meat that improves for hanging, and is at its best when eaten fresh. Personally, I prefer to skin them while they are still warm, but the Sahib prefers to do that job when the rabbit is quite cold. If it is fly season, watch out for the work of blowflies, which will lay their yellow eggs freely on your hard-won rabbits, especially around the head, rump and any areas with blood on them. To have brought your rabbits this far and then have them converted to a mass of maggots is not what you intended, unless you are a keen angler. I am told that rabbit skins come off easier if the carcase is frozen and then thawed, but it is not a good practice to then re-freeze them, so you might, like us, prefer to have them stored in the freezer ready for use. It is better not to freeze rabbits with the guts still in, as you can virtually guarantee that these will burst upon thawing. The only exception that I can think of is if you are providing rabbits for snake owners to feed their pets upon, when the snake prefers a whole carcase. Rabbits for birds of prey, ferrets and dogs need to be frozen as hygienically as for our own consumption. I have read about the old gamekeepers boiling rabbit carcases and feeding them whole to their dogs, and I can only think that they must have got through a lot of dogs, for rabbits have hard bones, and the structure of bones changes when they are cooked, making them more likely to splinter or else cause blockages in the gut. In the old days, rabbit was a big part of the diet of reared gamebirds, too, but this was cooked, taken off the bone and mixed with hard-boiled eggs and various cereals, usually with added secret ingredients according to the preferences of the headkeeper.

There is more than one way to skin a rabbit, but I will just cover the more usual methods. Now that the skin has no value, damage to it does not matter, so I start by using secateurs to cut the hindlegs off at the hock, and the forelegs off at the wrist. Dogs like to eat these, and will come to no harm by it. Then with the fingertips, extend the paunching gap upwards at the sides all the way to the backbone if you can do so without breaking the back. This is easy with tender young rabbits, but if you have a tough old customer, it can be a real struggle to part it from its skin. Start with the easy ones until you feel confident. Next, work the skin over one hindleg until you can pull the leg clear. Repeat the process with the other hindleg. The skin is now held on by the tail: if the rabbit is for human consumption, leave the tail for the moment and gently cut the skin away above it, but if it is dog food, cut through the tailbone and free the back part of the skin that way. Now gently pull the skin up over the foreparts of the rabbit, like a pullover, freeing the forelegs as you did the hind ones, until the skin is over the rabbit's neck. Cut through the neck, and save the head for the ferrets. You do not need to skin ferret food, and they benefit from the roughage of raw pelt and bone with their meat. Cooked meat is less good for ferrets, though still better than bread and milk, and as with dogs, never feed cooked bones. In the old days, people used to skin and eat the rabbit heads; Mrs Beeton considered this delicacy particularly good for invalids as it 'offers a variety of delicate pickings for the wayward appetite'. Times have changed, have they not?

Another way of skinning is to cut from the belly up the back of the rabbit right round to the other side, then slit along the backbone towards head and tail, and peel off in four pieces. If you have a particularly difficult rabbit to deal with, you may need to free the membrane between the skin and the flesh with the tip of your knife. If he was hard to skin, he will be tough to eat, and will need a different approach to cooking if you are preparing him for your own table.

If while skinning your bunny, you come across a sort of jelly bag under the skin, which can be the size of a golf ball or considerably bigger, these are tapeworm cysts. Do not touch with your bare hands! Destroy the skin and its inhabitants by burning; personally I do not use the rabbit either, but if you are desperate enough to need to use it, boil most thoroughly.

There will be times when you have so many rabbits that you do not relish the task of skinning each one, so skin up the back to the start of the ribcage and then cut through the spine. The fore end of the rabbit will do nicely for ferrets or birds of prey, and the best meat for you and your dogs is on the back and hindlegs. The fillet down either side of the spine is the nicest of all.

Assuming that you are preparing a whole rabbit for your own use, you have a little more to do. The rabbit has two scent glands either side of its tail, at the 'twenty to four' position, and these should be removed because otherwise the meat will taste strongly of rabbit musk, which many people find repugnant. These glands are bean-shaped, greyish-green, and just below the surface of the skin. If you pull up the tail, you will bring them up clearly, and then you can take them out with the tip of your knife. That is why you kept the tail on! You don't need it any more now, so cut if off, and split between the hindlegs so that you can get rid of any remaining plumbing and associated debris from the genital area. Cut the membrane that covers the end of the ribcage, and extract the heart and lungs. The ferrets will appreciate these, or you can add them to the dog-food stew. Rinse out all body cavities very thoroughly, and then put bunny to soak overnight in salt water. If you like, you can joint him before you do so, or after, or opt to cook him whole.

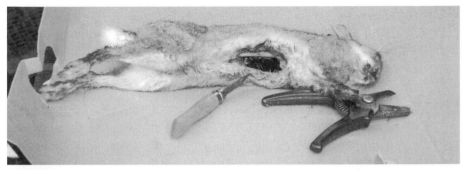

Ready to start . . .

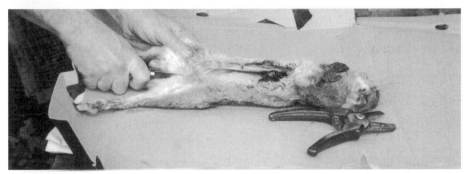

. . . extend paunching slit to between hindlegs . . .

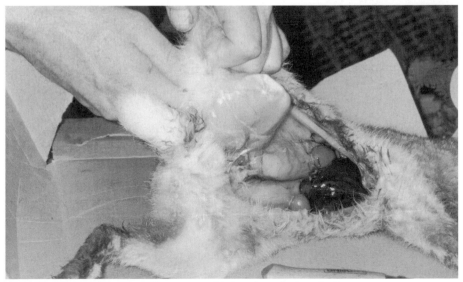

. . . free skin from hindleg, (note offset position of kidneys) . . . (and overleaf)

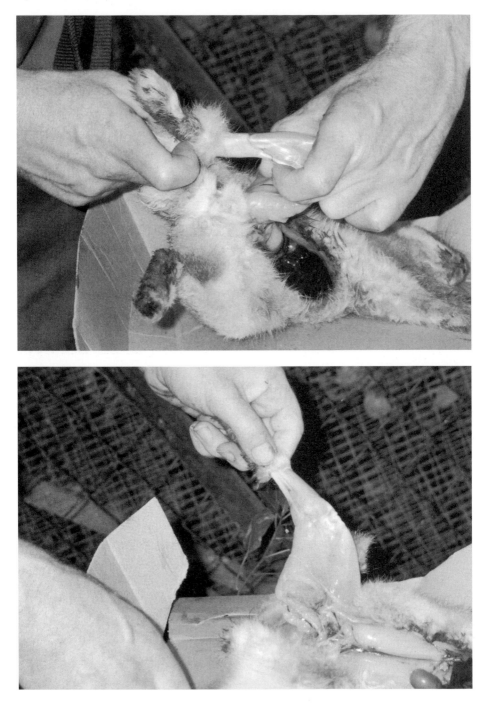

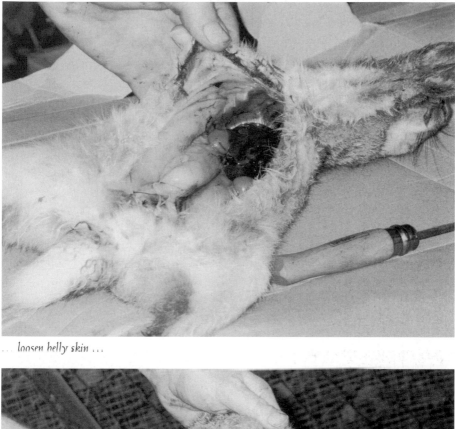

... loosen belly skin ...

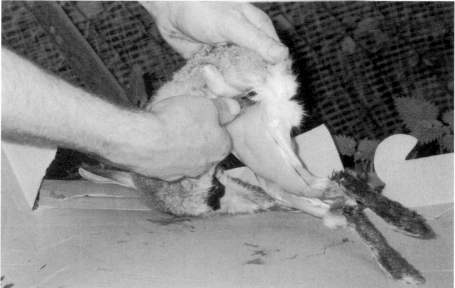

... free skin around tail ...

135

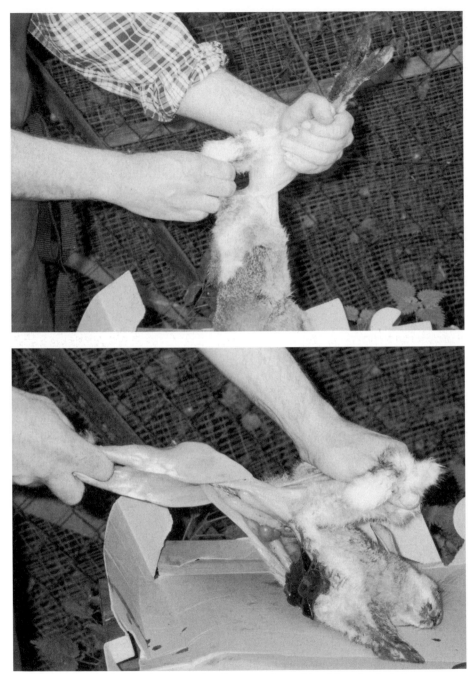

... pull skin forward (tail has been removed in these examples, and legs left on for clarity) ...

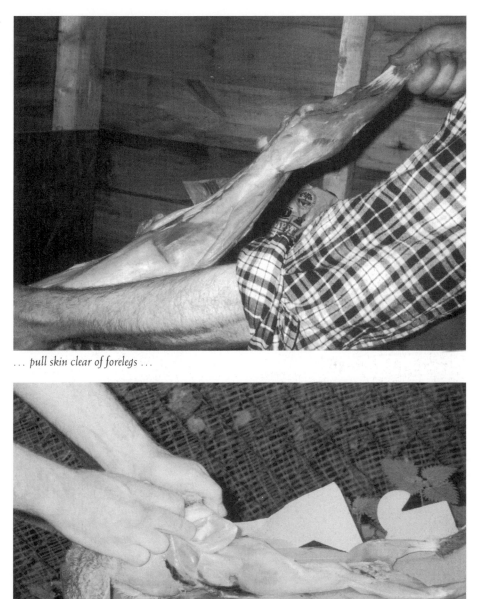

... pull skin clear of forelegs ...

... free forelegs ...

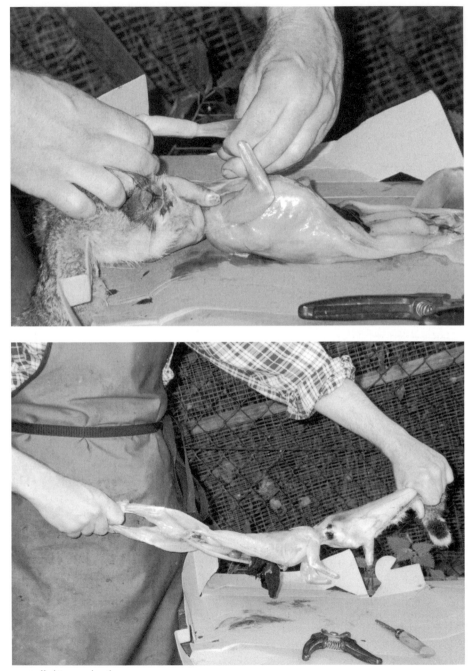

... pull skin over head ...

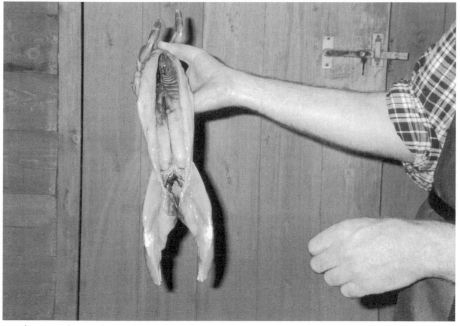

... clean out chest and genital cavities as shown

If you are jointing a whole rabbit, cut across in front of the hindlegs and then behind the ribcage, then along the spine to give two shoulder and two hindleg joints, plus the saddle. Another way, and good if the rabbit is small, is to leave the saddle attached to the foreparts of the rabbit. If the rabbit has been feeding on corn, it may carry a lot of bright yellow internal fat: this is quite harmless and will help lubricate the meat as it cooks. Well-fed on grassland tends to mean a creamer fat, and a lot of rabbits never eat well enough to have any fat on them at all. Very young rabbits are known here as 'fryers' and delicious simply fried in butter or olive oil. To tell a young full-grown rabbit from an old one, wiggle the feet to check for pliability, and squeeze at the elbow and stifle (knee) joints. Younger rabbits are flexible, the bones at the joints can be separately felt, and their ears tear more easily. If what you have is a hoary old Methuselah of a rabbit, you might like to take him from his salt bath, rinse him off thoroughly, and give him a few hours in milk as well. Some people prefer to soak their rabbits in milk anyway, rather than salt water. If a jelly-like membrane over most or all of the carcase becomes evident after soaking, this is not harmful but not wanted either, so remove it before cooking.

How shall I cook thee, let me count the ways! I have heard people say that rabbit tastes like chicken: believe me, it does not — it tastes just like rabbit. The texture of the meat is different, too. But it is a white meat, as distinct from hare, which is very dark and rich. Rabbit should be casseroled exquisitely slowly, with mushrooms and onions, and garlic if you like it. You can ring the changes with the taste by cooking in dry cider (my favourite) wine (red or white, but remember that wild rabbit has a robust flavour) or beer. A tin of tomatoes and some chopped celery will alter the flavour completely, or you can have old-fashioned rabbit stew with winter root vegetables, pearl barley and herb dumplings. The juice of an orange added to a basic rabbit hotpot goes well, and if you are feeling extravagant, squeeze in a couple of limes instead, but do not mix citrus with the tomatoes-and-celery option.

You will notice that I am not giving recipes as such, but an indication of tastes: this is because rabbit is an uncomplicated dish often cooked by people in a hurry. Just put everything into a lidded casserole dish or a pre-soaked earthenware cooking brick, add a knob of butter or a generous slosh of olive oil, a sprinkling of your favourite herbs, put into a hot oven for ten minutes or so, then turn down the heat, or if cooking on a range change ovens, and leave it to get on with cooking while you see to other jobs. Season with salt and black pepper, and a little cayenne or Worcester sauce will give some oomph on a cold day. If you want something a bit more fiddly, the French specialise in lovely velvety cream sauces, and also cook their *lapin* with prunes on occasion, which options are rather tasty. I once had rabbit and tripe cooked together in Portugal, which was much nicer than it sounds; it tasted as if a chicken stock had been involved. One or two pieces of fat pork, if you can get it, will transfer a rabbit dish into ambrosia, and a couple of pieces of oxtail added as an alternative may cause fighting to break out amongst your guests. In my opinion, there is only one thing to do with a tough old buck, if not fed to the dogs, and that is to curry it! Reckon on simmering it for the best part of the day, and don't forget the chutney. Cold rabbit forms a good jelly and is traditional as a pie, or as part of a game pie, or rabbit and ham is good together. A good country chutney and some pickled onions add to the pleasure, for rabbit can take any amount of strong flavours and come up smiling.

Unless you are a very special dog owner, cooking rabbit for dogs is obviously far less elaborate, and the usual method is to boil it until the meat comes easily off the bones. Warning – rabbit cooked this way stinks. Bluebottles and stray cats will come from miles around, and your best beloved (apart from the dogs) may leave home. If you add some apples to the cooking pot, it takes the sting out of the stench; if you add some chopped nettles, your dogs' coats will shine and often minor skin problems clear up. Best way to gather nettles is to scissor the young tops off into a bowl, and then tip them into the cooking pot; that way you do not have to touch them. You cannot overdo the apples and nettles, and a few other vegetables will do your dogs a lot of good as well. No onions for dogs, though, and only a little garlic as it can upset their stomachs quite dramatically. Garlic can make your hounds less appealing to parasites, but onions and dogs are not a good mix, even though some dogs really enjoy them. When you bone out the rabbit, be sure that you do not miss any of the small rib bones, and if the rabbits have been shot, be careful of bone splinters. You do not want them in your hand, and the dogs should not eat them. Pick out any obvious shot: our dogs are amazing at sifting out buckshot, but then lurchers are dainty eaters. I suspect more robust trenchers would just swallow the lot, and whereas small amounts of shot are unlikely to do any harm, your animals will be better off for not eating too much of it. Cats are very fond of rabbit, too, though no doubt they would prefer it unadorned with vegetable matter unless they are stealing it from the dogs bowls or the larder. Rabbit is easily digested, and welcomed by a sick animal that needs its appetite tempting. Rabbit broth is often easier taken than water, if your animal is tending to dehydration after a severe bout of diarrhoea and vomiting, and is a very good standby for invalid, very young or elderly animals.

Now you are the complete hunter-gatherer. You have found your rabbit, hunted it, caught it by whatever means, prepared, cooked and eaten it, and your ferrets, dogs and maybe cat are replete with rabbit also. Did the vegetables come from your garden as well? Treat yourself to feeling ineffably smug.

SALUTE

For those who do not know the rabbit, it is easy to underestimate him. He does not have the glamour or ferocity of larger game, his fur makes an inferior coat, and it is many generations since he was truly appreciated as a meal. Those who do not suffer directly from the damage he causes cannot appreciate his effect on the cost of the bread and vegetables that they buy, those who do not have to make good the results of his undermining could not begin to imagine the varied industries that have to include rabbit control in their annual budget.

Yet how much poorer we would be without him! Our wildflowers and insects, our very landscape is affected and often improved by him, our dogs glory in him, our marksmanship is challenged by him. He teaches us patience, thoroughness, neatness, observation and the relationship between cause and effect as we strive to catch him: he teaches us fieldcraft, silence, concealment, and harmony with the natural world. We will never eradicate him, nor should we want to. The sporting rabbit offers a constant challenge to those of us who seek to meet him on his own terms in his own territory (did you think it was your land? It is undeniably his as well). Through these pages, we have explored the human response to the rabbit's presence, his damage and his usefulness. In going out and hunting him yourself, you will not only be performing a proper and necessary service, you will be learning much about your own ways and perceptions, and without doubt be the richer for it. For all his destructive ways, the rabbit has done the same for all who are willing to learn from him. Certainly, without the dogs and ferrets, the old friends and the new skills, the farms and estates, the dawns and dusks and stormy nights that have entered my life as a direct result of hunting the rabbit, my life would have been far less colourful. Whatever the complexities and frustrations of human 'civilisation', an hour or two spent rabbiting will put everything in perspective. Ladies and Gentlemen, I give you a toast: The Rabbit!

APPENDICES

Bibliography

Ground Game, M. Brander (Tideline Books, 1978)
The Ways of the Warrener, Pat Carey (Warrener Productions, 1999)
The Rabbit, James Edward Harting (Ashford Press, 1986)
Rabbiting, Bob Smithson (Crowood Press, 1988)
The Private Life of the Rabbit, R.M. Lockley (André Deutsch, 1954)
Pugs and Drummers, John Marchington (Faber and Faber, 1978)
Rabbits and Hares, Anne McBride (Whittet Books, 1988)
Fair Game, Charlie Parkes and John Thornley (Pelham Books, 1987)
In Pursuit of Coney, D. Brian Plummer (Boydell Press, 1991)
Rabbits and their History, John Sheail, (Readers' Union, 1972)
Rabbit Shooting to Ferrets, William Thomas (Tideline Books, 1979)

Useful Addresses

British Association for Shooting and Conservation, Marford Mill, Rossett, Wrexham LL12 OHL (01244 573000) www.basc.org.uk
The Countryside Alliance, The Old Town Hall, 367 Kennington Road, London SE11 4PT (020 7840 9200) www.countryside-alliance.org (this isn't a mistake: there is nothing after the 'org'.)
The Countryman's Weekly, Unit 2 Lynher House, 3 Bush Park, Estover, Plymouth, Devon PL6 7RG (01822 855281) www.countrymansweekly.co.uk
The Game Conservancy Trust (Registered Charity no.279968) Fordingbridge, Hampshire SP6 1EF (01245 652381)
http://www.game-conservancy.org.uk/
Scottish Countryside Alliance, Royal Highland Showground, East Gate, Ingliston, Midlothian EH28 8NF (0131 335 0200)
www.scottishcountrysidealliance.org

Index

Agriculture, Ministry of 16, 17, 40
Australia 15, 16, 17, 36, 40-1

Backnetting 57, 120
Blink reflex 126
Bobbery pack 18, 75, 83-5
Breeding, rabbits 27, 28, 29 34
Bushing 73-5

Calicivirus, rabbit 17, 36, 40-1
Chinning, how to 123-4

Damage, by rabbits 12-3, 18, 25, 35, 101, 119
Delille, Armand 16, 40
Despatch, of rabbits 55, 95, 122-6
Dogs, rabbiting 31, 55-8, 59-60, 73-87, 95-6, 116, 117, 121, 142
Draining, rabbits 126, 128

Feet, rabbit 32, 34
Fencing, rabbit 116-9, 121
Ferret 21, 42-63, 70, 78, 79, 121, 122, 129, 132, 142
Fleas, rabbit 16, 17, 22, 36
Fly-strike 11

Game Laws 11, 19
Garden rabbits 110, 112, 120-1
Gas, use of 114-6, 121
Gutting see Paunching

Hawk 18, 43, 59-60, 62, 122

Head, buck 29
Head, doe 28
Hocking 126-7

Lamping, dog 71, 72, 79-83

Lamping, equipment 81-2
Lamping, rifle 64, 68-72
Line ferret 44
Locator, ferret 44-6
Long-net 18, 50, 59, 73, 79, 88-99, 125
Lurcher 31, 45, 55-8, 72, 77-82, 84-7, 141

Mange, sarcoptic 15
Mutation, virus 17, 39-41
Myxomatosis 15, 16, 17, 21, 22, 29, 36-41

Necking see Despatch
Noises, rabbit 29-30

Paunching 19, 44, 72, 128-130
Purse nets 18, 49-50, 52

Repellents 119-120
Roundworms 25

Sea Ferret 63
Shooting, air rifle 65-7
        rifle 18, 64-72, 77
        rough 75-6, 78
        shotgun 18, 60-2, 64, 72, 75
Skinning 18, 131-9
Snares 100-3, 122
Stinking Out 120
Stop-nets 50, 59, 98

Tapeworms 25, 26-7, 129, 132
Teeth, rabbit 24-5, 30, 34
Trapping 18, 100-113, 121

Viral Haemorrhagic
Disease see Calicivirus